I Exalt
You,
O GOD

Encountering His Greatness
in Your Private Worship

JERRY BRIDGES

WATERBROOK
PRESS

I EXALT YOU, O GOD
PUBLISHED BY WATERBROOK PRESS
2375 Telstar Drive, Suite 160
Colorado Springs, Colorado 80920
A division of Random House, Inc.

ISBN 1-57856-421-2

Library of Congress Cataloging-in-Publication Data
Bridges, Jerry.
  I exalt you, O God : encountering His greatness in your private worship / Jerry Bridges.— 1st ed.
    p. cm.
  Includes bibliographical references and index.
  ISBN 1-57856-421-2
  1. God—Worship and love. I. Title.

BV4817 .B67 2001
248.3—dc21

00-043871

Printed in the United States of America
2001—First Edition

10 9 8 7 6 5 4 3 2 1

CONTENTS

Therefore, since we are receiving
a kingdom that cannot be shaken,
let us be thankful, and so worship God acceptably
with reverence and awe,
for our "God is a consuming fire."

HEBREWS 12:28-29

HE IS WORTHY

What is worship?

In Scripture the word *worship* is used to denote both an overall way of life and a specific activity. When the prophet Jonah said, "I am a Hebrew and I worship the LORD, the God of heaven, who made the sea and the land" (Jonah 1:9), he was speaking of his whole manner of life.

In contrast to Jonah's words, Psalm 100:2 says, "Worship the LORD with gladness; come before him with joyful songs." The psalmist there speaks of a specific activity of praising God. This is the sense in which we normally use the word *worship* today.

These two concepts of worship—a broad one and a more narrow, specific one—correspond to the two ways by which we glorify God. We glorify God by ascribing to Him the honor and adoration due Him because of His excellence—the narrow concept of worship. We also glorify God by reflecting His glory to others—the broader, way-of-life manner of worship.

WORSHIP AS A WAY OF LIFE

Look at how this broader concept is taught in a familiar verse from Paul: "Therefore, I urge you, brothers, in view of God's mercy, to offer your bodies as living sacrifices, holy and pleasing to God—this is your spiritual act of worship" (Romans 12:1). To offer our bodies as living sacrifices is to worship God. That Paul intended not just the physical body, but one's entire being, is implied from Romans 6:13, where he speaks of offering ourselves to God and the parts of our bodies to Him as instruments of righteousness.

To offer your body to God necessarily involves offering your mind, emotions, and will to Him also. It is the whole-hearted dedication to God of heart, mind, will, words, and deeds—in fact all that you are, have, and do. It is a total way of life. Paul called that our spiritual act of worship. John Calvin had this comprehensive sense of worship in mind when he described the worship of God as "the beginning and foundation of righteousness."[1]

To attempt to worship God in only the narrow sense of praising Him without also seeking to worship Him in our whole way of life is hypocrisy. Jesus rebuked the Pharisees because they were going through outward motions of worship, but their hearts were not committed to God. "You hypocrites!" He said. "Isaiah was right when he prophesied about you: 'These people honor me with their lips, but their hearts are far from me. They worship me in vain; their teachings are but rules taught by men'" (Matthew 15:7-9).

This book is intended to encourage your worship in the more limited definition of that word, but it's important to understand that a lifestyle of worship is the necessary foundation for all our praise and adoration, both privately and corporately.

THE GLORY DUE GOD'S NAME

What really is this worship, in the sense of praise and adoration?

The Puritan Stephen Charnock called it "nothing else but a rendering to God the honor that is due him."[2]

John MacArthur defined it as "honor and adoration directed to God."[3]

A. W. Tozer gave a more expanded meaning. He said that God "wants to cultivate within us the adoration and admiration of which He is worthy. He wants us to be astonished at the inconceivable elevation and magnitude and splendor of Almighty God!"[4]

One of the best biblical descriptions of worship is Psalm 29:1-2.

Ascribe to the LORD, O mighty ones,
ascribe to the LORD glory and strength.

> *Ascribe to the LORD the glory due his name;*
>   *worship the LORD in the splendor of his holiness.*

This is the essence of worship: *Ascribe to the Lord the glory due His name.* Before we can do that, we must understand something of the glory that is due Him. We have to begin grasping His greatness, holiness, wisdom, and love, which is what the thirty-one daily readings in this book are designed to help you do. We must meditate on and pray over the kind of passages mentioned in this book, such as Isaiah 6:1-8, Isaiah 40, Daniel 4:34-35, Psalm 104, and 1 John 4:8-10. (Each of this book's daily sections concludes with a prayer to serve as an example and springboard for your own praying of Scripture in private worship. You may want to read these aloud as a personal expression of worship to God.)

In order to render heartfelt worship to God, we must be gripped in the depth of our being by His majesty, holiness, and love; otherwise our praise and adoration may be no more than empty words. Isn't this one reason why much of our worship today is so anemic and heartless?

But we can encounter God in His Word as we meditate on it and pray over it, asking the Holy Spirit to reveal to our hearts the glory of God as seen in His infinite attributes. We must do this if we're to worship God in a manner of which He is worthy.

Heartfelt Thanksgiving

It has been said that we praise God for *who* He is and thank Him for what He *does* for us. Such a precise distinction between praise and thanksgiving probably isn't wise, but the statement does call our attention to the fact that thanksgiving is an important aspect of worship.

Luke's account of ten lepers who cried out to Jesus to heal them is an insightful story that helps us see how important thanksgiving is to our worship. Jesus told them, "Go show yourselves to the priests." As they went on their way, they were healed.

> *One of them, when he saw he was healed, came back, praising God in a loud voice. He threw himself at Jesus' feet and thanked him—and he was a Samaritan.*
>
> *Jesus asked, "Were not all ten cleansed? Where are the other nine? Was no one found to return and give praise to God except this foreigner?" (Luke 17:15-18)*

Ten were cleansed; only one returned to give thanks. Jesus emphasized the uncalled-for disparity between the many and the one: *Where were the other nine?* The lesson is obvious. God does note when we take time to thank Him and when we don't.

I believe God also takes note of the sincerity and depth

of meaning we put into giving thanks to Him. Being healed of leprosy—or of cancer in our time—is vastly less significant than having eternal life. If we had to choose between being healed of cancer and receiving eternal life, the decision for any Christian would be easy. Yet how often do we express our thanksgiving to God for the gift of eternal life with as much depth of feeling as the one leper who "came back, praising God in a loud voice" and who "threw himself at Jesus' feet and thanked him"?

It's difficult to separate thanksgiving from praise in our worship of God. A better practice is to join them, as we see in Psalm 100:

> *Enter his gates with thanksgiving*
> *and his courts with praise;*
> *give thanks to him and praise his name.*
> *For the LORD is good and his love endures forever;*
> *his faithfulness continues through all generations.*
> *(verses 4-5)*

RECOGNIZING GOD'S OWNERSHIP

Praise and thanksgiving are also combined in David's beautiful prayer of worship as recorded in 1 Chronicles 29:10-14, on the occasion of the people's generous and wholehearted giving toward the building of the temple.

David praised the LORD in the presence of the whole assembly, saying,

"Praise be to you, O LORD,
    God of our father Israel,
    from everlasting to everlasting.
Yours, O LORD, is the greatness and the power
    and the glory and the majesty and the splendor,
    for everything in heaven and earth is yours.
Yours, O LORD, is the kingdom;
    you are exalted as head over all.
Wealth and honor come from you;
    you are the ruler of all things.
In your hands are strength and power
    to exalt and give strength to all.
Now, our God, we give you thanks,
    and praise your glorious name.

"But who am I, and who are my people, that we should be able to give as generously as this? Everything comes from you, and we have given you only what comes from your hand."

David began by praising God for His surpassing glory. Note how he heaps up words of praise and adulation: *greatness, power, glory, majesty,* and *splendor.* David was not simply being eloquent. He was pouring forth heartfelt praise in recognition of God's sovereignty: "You are exalted as head over all."

He was also acknowledging something that lies at the heart of the fear of God, and thus provides the basis for our appropriate worship of Him: The recognition that God is the ultimate owner of everything, and that we are only stewards of that which He has given to us. It is a recognition of our dependence upon Him and our responsibility to Him.

David said in Psalm 24:1, "The earth is the LORD's, and everything in it, the world, and all who live in it." In reality, all of us—even the wealthiest people in the world—are like the poorest peasants in the world's most disadvantaged nation. God owns everything; we own nothing.

In fact, according to David, we don't even own ourselves. Not only does *everything* in the world belong to God, but also *all who live in it.* This is doubly true for the Christian, for as Paul says in 1 Corinthians 6:19-20, "You are not your own; you were bought at a price." God owns us first by creation and again by redemption.

Job was a man who, according to the testimony of God Himself, feared God (Job 1:8). He was also a very wealthy man, "the greatest man among all the people of the East" (Job 1:3). We know how God allowed Satan to attack Job so that he lost all of his children and all of his possessions in a single day. How did Job respond?

Job got up and tore his robe and shaved his head. Then he
fell to the ground in worship and said:

"Naked I came from my mother's womb,
*   and naked I will depart.*
The LORD gave and the LORD has taken away;
*   may the name of the LORD be praised."*

In all this, Job did not sin by charging God with
wrongdoing. (Job 1:20-22)

Job's response was to worship God by acknowledging
that God was really the owner of all that he possessed and
that God had a right both to give and to take away. Conse-
quently, Job did not become angry at God and charge Him
with wrongdoing. Instead he worshiped God because he
feared Him.

YOUR PRIVATE WORSHIP

Both private and corporate worship—that which we do
individually and that which we do with other believers—are
taught in Scripture. For example, David says in Psalm
69:30, "I will praise God's name in song and glorify him
with thanksgiving." Here David refers to his own personal
worship. Again in Psalm 86:12, he says, "I will praise you,
O Lord my God, with all my heart; I will glorify your name

forever." This particular example of David's private worship follows immediately after his prayer that God would give him an undivided heart to fear His name (verse 11).

The vitality and genuineness of corporate worship is to a large degree dependent upon the vitality of our individual private worship. If we aren't spending time daily worshiping God, we're not apt to contribute to the corporate experience of worship. If we aren't worshiping God during the week, how can we expect to genuinely participate in it on Sunday morning? We may indeed go through the motions and think we have worshiped, but how can we honor and adore One on Sunday whom we have not taken time to praise and give thanks to during the week?

I agree with John MacArthur, who wrote:

> *Music and liturgy can assist or express a worshiping heart, but they cannot make a non-worshiping heart into a worshiping one. The danger is that they can give a non-worshiping heart the sense of having worshiped.*
>
> *So the crucial factor in worship in the church is not the form of worship, but the state of the hearts of the saints. If our corporate worship isn't the expression of our individual worshiping lives, it is unacceptable. If you think you can live any way you want and then go to church on Sunday morning and turn on worship with the saints, you're wrong.*[5]

In contrast to the once-a-week worshiper (and that term itself is an oxymoron), David worshiped God continually. "I will extol the LORD at *all* times," he said; "his praise will *always* be on my lips" (Psalm 34:1).

Again in Psalm 145:1-2 he told God:

I will exalt you, my God the King;
    I will praise your name for ever and ever.
Every day *I will praise you*
    and extol your name for ever and ever.

He goes on to say, "Great is the LORD and most worthy of praise; his greatness no one can fathom" (verse 3). In these words we sense the depth of his feeling, an emotion that could not be "pumped up" with a once-a-week visit to the house of God.

WORSHIP IN SPIRIT

Jesus spelled out the first essential of worship when He said to the Samaritan woman, "God is spirit, and his worshipers must worship in spirit and in truth" (John 4:24).

The "spirit" in which Jesus says we must worship God is the human spirit. It is what Paul often refers to as the heart. Worship is not just an external act. True worship must come from the heart and reflect a sincere attitude and desire.

"Without the heart," Stephen Charnock wrote,

it is no worship; it is a stage play, an acting a part with-out being that person really which is acted by us: a hypo-crite, in the notion of the word, is a stage player.... We may be truly said to worship God, though we [lack] per-fection; but we cannot be said to worship him if we [lack] sincerity.[6]

Jesus said we must also worship "in truth." Our worship must be in harmony with what God has revealed about Himself in His Word. It is possible to have zeal without knowledge (Romans 10:2). For example, if we stress only one side of God's attributes—say, His mercy and love—without also stressing His sovereignty and holiness, we're not worshiping in truth.

ENTER BY THE BLOOD OF JESUS

A second essential in worship is that we must always come to God through Christ. Paul is explicit about this: "*In him* and *through faith in him* we may approach God with freedom and confidence" (Ephesians 3:12); "For *through him* we both [Jews and Gentiles alike] have access to the Father by one Spirit" (2:18). And having come through Christ, we can approach God with confidence: "We have confidence to enter the Most Holy Place by the blood of Jesus" (Hebrews 10:19).

In the Old Testament era there were three restrictions on entering God's Most Holy Place in the temple: *Only* the high priest could enter, and *only* once a year, and *only* with the blood of atonement (Hebrews 9:7). But now, says the writer to the Hebrews, all believers may enter. In fact we have *confidence* to enter, which implies free and continuous access.

So two restrictions have been removed, while one remains: *We still must come by the blood.* Only now it is not the blood of a goat, but the blood of Jesus. Though we have been born again, and though our sins—past, present, and future—have been forgiven, we must still approach God through the merit of Jesus Christ. We are never of ourselves worthy to come before a holy God.

Nineteenth-century theologian Archibald Alexander composed a devotional exercise, apparently for his own private use, that included these words:

> *I am deeply convinced that my best duties have fallen far short of the perfection of Thy law, and have been so mingled with sin in the performance, that I might justly be condemned for the most fervent prayer I ever made.*[7]

Dr. Alexander's observation about himself is true of every one of us. Because of the continued presence of indwelling sin in our hearts and because of our consequent lack of perfect obedience, we are never, of ourselves, worthy to come into the presence of God and worship. We must always come through Christ. Our "spiritual sacrifices," as Peter said, are "acceptable to God *through Jesus Christ*" (1 Peter 2:5).

The writer of Hebrews taught this same truth: "*Through Jesus,* therefore, let us continually offer to God a sacrifice of praise—the fruit of lips that confess his name" (Hebrews 13:15). It is always through Jesus that we offer to God a sacrifice of praise. Our most fervent expressions of worship, either in prayer or song, are unacceptable to God if they are not offered through His Son.

CHERISH NO SIN

A third essential to worship is a heart free from cherished sin. David said, "If I had cherished sin in my heart, the Lord would not have listened" (Psalm 66:18). To cherish a sin is to hold on to some sinful disposition or course of action we know is wrong. Perhaps you have been wronged by someone, and you know you should forgive as the Lord forgave you. Yet you are unwilling to let go of that unforgiving spirit. Instead you cherish it and nourish it. You cannot truly worship God when you are in that state.

Perhaps you are involved in some unethical business practice that may be barely legal but does not meet the test of love, of treating others as you would like to be treated.

In your innermost heart you know the practice is wrong but you're unwilling to give it up because of the financial cost. Or perhaps you love to gossip. The Holy Spirit has convicted you of it many times, but you enjoy it. You get a perverse delight out of running down other people because it makes you feel good about yourself. If you're resisting the convicting work of the Holy Spirit, you are cherishing sin in your heart, and you cannot truly worship God.

Let me emphasize that there's a difference between struggling with sin and cherishing it. You may genuinely desire to forgive another person. In your mind you have said many times, "I forgive her," yet your own corrupt heart keeps bringing it up. You cry out to God to change you, but for some reason He allows you to keep struggling. That is not cherishing sin; that is warring against it. What you need to do in that case is to appropriate the blood of Christ to cleanse your conscience so you may worship freely (see Hebrews 9:14).

HELP IN OUR WORSHIP

Perhaps the idea of private worship is new to you. You have always thought of worship as something to do on Sunday morning at church with other believers. Now you see the importance of private, daily worship, but you don't know how to begin.

Of course the first thing you have to do is select a time. I have my personal worship in conjunction with my daily Bible reading and prayer, which I do each day before breakfast. I begin my prayer with words designed to capture both the awe and the intimacy with which we should relate to God. I consciously and deliberately enter into His presence through the merit of Christ, acknowledging my sinfulness, pleading His cleansing blood, and confessing that only through Christ can I call God my Father.

The joy of realizing my sins are forgiven and that I am accepted by the Father through Christ lifts my soul to praise and thanksgiving. I often use a biblical prayer of praise such as David's in 1 Chronicles 29:10-14. I take time to thank God for my salvation and for the way He has led in my Christian life throughout the years. I consider where I could have been had God not intervened in my life at various points.

I reflect on my humble beginnings as a child growing up during the depression years in a working-class family and consider where God has brought me. I think of Jacob's words that describe so accurately my own life's story: "I am unworthy of all the kindness and faithfulness you have shown your servant. I had only my staff when I crossed this Jordan, but now I have become two groups" (Genesis 32:10). I acknowledge my absolute dependence on God for life and daily provision. I thank Him for a godly wife and for children who follow Him.

As I read the Bible, I often come across passages of Scripture that remind me of some truth about God, or perhaps even reveal to me something new. When that happens I pause once again and worship.

Sometimes I use a book titled *The Valley of Vision,* a collection of Puritan prayers and devotions, to stimulate my own sense of praise. Here's an example:

GREAT GOD,
In public and private, in sanctuary and home,
     may my life be steeped in prayer,
     filled with the spirit of grace and supplication,
     each prayer perfumed with the incense of atoning
          blood.
Help me, defend me, until from praying ground
I pass to the realm of unceasing praise.
Urged by my need,
Invited by thy promises,
Called by thy Spirit,
I enter thy presence, worshiping thee with godly fear,
     awed by thy majesty, greatness, glory,
     but encouraged by thy love.
I am all poverty as well as all guilt,
     having nothing of my own with which to repay thee,
But I bring Jesus to thee in the arms of faith,
     pleading His righteousness to offset my iniquities,

rejoicing that he will weigh down the scales for me,
and satisfy thy justice.
I bless thee that great sin draws out great grace,
that although the least sin deserves infinite
punishment
because done against an infinite God,
yet there is mercy for me,
for where guilt is most terrible,
there thy mercy in Christ is most free and deep.
Bless me by revealing to me more of his saving merits,
by causing thy goodness to pass before me,
by speaking peace to my contrite heart;
Strengthen me to give thee no rest
until Christ shall reign supreme within me,
in every thought, word, and deed,
in a faith that purifies the heart,
overcomes the world, works by love,
fastens me to thee, and ever clings to the cross.[8]

Some people use hymns as a part of their daily worship. A. W. Tozer kept a stack of hymn books in his study for that purpose. Other people use one of many devotional books available. Whatever helps you and is biblical, you should use. The important thing is that you worship God in spirit and truth.

"LORD, I AM WILLING"

Our submission to God is also an important part of worship. We've already seen this demonstrated in the life of Job when he submitted to God's providential dealings. (Although Satan was the agent of Job's trials, their ultimate cause is attributed to God Himself [see Job 1:21 and 42:11]).

After the death of my first wife, a friend passed on to me a little saying by an unknown author that helps me express my submission to God:

> *Lord, I am willing*
> *To receive what You give;*
> *To lack what You withhold;*
> *To relinquish what You take;*
> *To suffer what You inflict;*
> *To be what You require.*

I keep a copy of this in my prayer notebook and pray over it several times a week. I've also added another sentence: "And to do what You send me to do."

Our posture in worship is also important. Old Testament passages that speak of worship often speak of bowing down. For example, Psalm 95:6 says, "Come, let us bow down in worship, let us kneel before the LORD our Maker" (see also Deuteronomy 8:19; 2 Chronicles 20:18 and 29:28; Job 1:20; Ephesians 3:14; Revelation 22:8).

Kneeling or bowing down is a physical expression of reverence and submission. I don't want to imply that you must always bow down to worship effectively, though I think we should do it frequently. The important thing is your attitude of heart. I often do my Bible reading and part of my worship sitting at our dining table. Because of a peculiar deformity in my lower backbone, I'm more comfortable if I slouch down in my chair. When I pause to worship, however, I like to sit up straight with both feet on the floor. Even though this is uncomfortable, I want to do it as a sign of reverence to God.

GROWING IN WORSHIP

I've offered here a number of suggestions and principles for your private worship. If we're to benefit from them we must ask ourselves some hard questions:

1. Have I presented myself and all that I have to God as a living sacrifice, so that my way of life is a life of worship?
2. Do I take time daily to worship God privately and to thank Him for all His blessings to me?
3. Is there some "cherished" sin, some practice I'm unwilling to give up, that hinders my worship?

4. Do I seek to enter wholeheartedly and "in spirit and truth" into worship? Or do I simply go through the motions without really worshiping?

None of us will score perfectly on these questions. That is not their intent. Rather they're designed to help us honestly assess ourselves and pinpoint areas of our lives that need improvement. Only then, and as we take steps to improve, will this book be of benefit to us.

Part I

For Your Greatness, O God, I Exalt You

Oh, praise the greatness of our God!

Deuteronomy 32:3

Consider what great things he has done for you.

1 Samuel 12:24

How awesome are your deeds!
So great is your power that your enemies cringe before you.
All the earth bows down to you; they sing praise to you,
they sing praise to your name.

Psalm 66:3-4

GOD PLAYS FOR KEEPS

The narrative parts of the Old Testament often read like an adventure novel. Many of the stories really are high drama. What could be more suspenseful than Daniel in the lions' den or his three friends in the blazing furnace? What could be more romantic than the aggrieved Gentile woman Ruth meeting her future husband, Boaz, while gleaning in his grainfield, and ultimately becoming an ancestor of both Israel's King David and Jesus the Messiah?

These and numerous other classic stories can lull us into the attitude that what we're reading is hardly more than good fiction.

Reinforcing that tendency is the abundance in these stories of miraculous events that seem so unreal today. We don't read in our newspapers of someone killing a thousand men with a donkey's jawbone, as Samson did. We don't hear about floating axheads, or a family living for months on only a handful of flour and a little jug of oil.

Though entertaining, these events can seem so far back and foreign that we unconsciously view them as having no practical value today. Yet if the Bible is indeed God's Word, we know these amazing stories are authentic accounts of real events happening to real people like you and me.

Of all the astonishing miracles recorded in the Old Testament, the most momentous for the Jews was their crossing of the Red Sea. To display His glory and destroy Pharaoh's army, God directed the Israelites to a location where they were penned in between the sea and the Egyptians. The Scriptures tell us that when the Israelites looked up and saw Pharaoh's elite forces marching after them, they were terrified and complained bitterly against Moses for bringing them out into the desert to die (Exodus 14).

To appreciate their predicament, imagine being finally delivered from slavery, only to see your former masters in hot pursuit and no way of escape. What emotions would surge through you as you faced this extreme danger—and later as you experienced miraculous deliverance?

Imagine seeing the Red Sea waters divided, opening a way for you and two million others to walk through on dry ground. You step down into the sea bottom with those walls of water towering above. Could they at any moment come crashing down?

At last you reach the far side, only to look back and see that the Egyptians have followed. Suddenly you watch those walls of water collapse; you witness an entire army drowning in the sea. In only a few hours you've experienced the highest degrees of fear, apprehension, dismay, excitement, and overwhelming relief.

However, the Israelites experienced something more than relief and elation following the climax of that day's events: "And when the Israelites saw the great power the LORD displayed against the Egyptians, the people feared the LORD and put their trust in him and in Moses his servant" (Exodus 14:31).

The people feared the Lord. Obviously this wasn't the same fear or dread they felt upon seeing the fast-approaching Egyptian army. Rather it was the reverential awe produced by the awesome display of God's might. While they rejoiced that this power had been exercised in their behalf, they could not escape the sober realization that this God was not only an almighty deliverer, but also a righteous judge of those who opposed Him. As a friend of mine put it, they realized that God plays for keeps.

The text says that the Israelites both feared the Lord *and* put their trust in Him. Fearing God and trusting Him are not mutually exclusive. In fact, the Israelites were able to trust God *because* they experienced firsthand His awesome power to deliver them. It was not just the display of raw power—the Egyptians also saw that—but the exercise of it *in their behalf* that caused the Hebrews to trust God. Power without love is terrifying. Love without power is pitiable. In God the Jews saw both working together.

O mighty God, my loving Father, I praise and thank You for acting so strongly on my behalf both to save me and to transform me.

This I know: "that God is for me"; and since You are for me, who can be against me? Therefore, "in God I trust; I will not be afraid." Romans 8:31; Psalm 56:9-11

You have commanded me to trust You with all my heart and to lean not on my own understanding. You have promised that "in quietness and trust" is my strength, and that You will keep me in perfect peace as I steadfastly trust in You. Proverbs 3:5; Isaiah 30:15; 26:3

So I bring to You my faith: "In you I trust, O my God." "I trust in you, O LORD; I say, 'You are my God.'" "I will say of the LORD, 'He is my refuge and my fortress, my God, in whom I trust.'" Psalms 25:2; 31:14; 91:2

"O LORD Almighty, blessed is the man who trusts in you." I praise and thank You for those words of promise, for by Your grace I believe that this very blessing shall also be mine. Psalm 84:12

TO FEAR HIM IS
TO TRUST HIM

It's apparent that God's aim in the events of the Exodus was not only to gain glory to Himself, but also to stimulate and increase the faith of the Israelites. He deliberately maneuvered them into a situation where they could be saved only by His mighty power, and through that experience come to trust Him.

A similar relationship between the fear of the Lord and trust in Him is expressed in Psalm 33:16-19.

No king is saved by the size of his army;
*   no warrior escapes by his great strength.*
A horse is a vain hope for deliverance;
*   despite all its great strength it cannot save.*
But the eyes of the LORD are on those who fear him,
*   on those whose hope is in his unfailing love,*
to deliver them from death
*   and keep them alive in famine.*

Note that the passage begins by expressing the vanity of trust in such earthly things as an army, one's own strength, or even the strength of a horse (the equivalent of a modern army's tank). Instead we're encouraged to fear the Lord and to hope in His unfailing love—that is, to trust Him.

But why should we fear and trust Him? What basis do we have for doing so? The answer has already been given in the preceding verses:

> *By the word of the LORD were the heavens made,*
>> *their starry host by the breath of his mouth.*
> *He gathers the waters of the sea into jars;*
>> *he puts the deep into storehouses.*
> *Let all the earth fear the LORD;*
>> *let all the people of the world revere him.*
> *For he spoke, and it came to be;*
>> *he commanded, and it stood firm.*
> *The LORD foils the plans of the nations;*
>> *he thwarts the purposes of the peoples.*
> *But the plans of the LORD stand firm forever,*
>> *the purposes of his heart through all generations.*
>> *(verses 6-11)*

This passage extols first God's power in creation and later His sovereignty over the nations. Right in the middle we're exhorted to fear the Lord and revere Him, or as other translations say, "Fear the LORD and stand in awe of him." And what will cause us to do so? It is recognizing His greatness as displayed in His mighty power in creation and His absolute sovereignty over the nations. As we become convinced of His greatness, we will fear Him—stand in awe of Him—and also trust Him.

The eyes of my heart are on You, O Lord, as I celebrate Your mighty power displayed in creation and Your absolute sovereignty over the nations.

Convinced of Your greatness, I fear You and stand in awe of You. Because I fear You, I trust You; and because I trust You, I worship You. "You are worthy, our Lord and God, to receive glory and honor and power, for you created all things, and by your will they were created and have their being." Revelation 4:11

Fearing You is "the beginning of wisdom," and the beginning as well of my worship. "Who is like you...awesome in glory?" No one is! "You alone are to be feared." "You alone are God." So You alone I worship. Psalm 111:10; Exodus 15:11; Psalms 76:7; 86:10

Let my worship be acceptable to You today, O living God. Hebrews 12:22,28

HE IS INFINITELY GREAT

Sadly enough, we have only to read the history of the Hebrews to realize how poorly they learned to fear Him. Psalm 78 is a dismal account of how Israel continually sinned against God by failing to trust Him. Verse 32 says that "in spite of his wonders, they did not believe." They did not trust God because they did not stand in awe of Him and of the wonders He often performed in their behalf.

Like the Jewish nation, we, too, need to grow in the fear of God, lest we also sin against Him by failing to trust Him. One problem we have, however, is that God seldom displays His mighty power in such spectacular ways as He did for Israel. This isn't to say God isn't powerfully at work today, but most often He has chosen to carry out His purposes and to work in behalf of His people through seemingly ordinary events.

How then can we grow in the fear of God when we don't see Him performing miracles? One way is by regularly reading through the Old Testament (particularly the historical sections and the Psalms), reminding ourselves that the same God who performed those mighty acts still reigns and rules over His creation and is still working on behalf of His people.

When I was in high school my parents struggled to make ends meet, and there was no way they could have helped me with the expenses of a college education. After graduation I planned to go to the local junior college for two years and see what might happen from there. One evening during my senior year I discovered inside our newspaper a single-column article no more than four inches long. It mentioned a navy scholarship program that provided a college education and an officer's commission upon graduation. I applied, passed the examination, and was accepted.

The seemingly "chance" reading of that article buried in our newspaper was literally a life-changing event. My education, my contact with the Navigators while on active duty, and my subsequent Christian ministry all hinged upon it. Why did I "happen" to see it? Because God was at work on my behalf carrying out His plan for me.

My little experience was certainly not as dramatic as the Israelites crossing the Red Sea, but in some respects it was as life changing. It also demonstrated that God is just as much at work now on behalf of His people as He was in Old Testament times.

For the awesomeness that God displays in His mighty acts, the Scriptures often use the word *great* or *greatness*. In the song Moses composed immediately after the Red Sea crossing, he says, "In the *greatness* of your majesty you threw down those who opposed you" (Exodus 15:7). Moses also refers to the Lord as "a *great* and awesome God" and as "the *great* God, mighty and awesome" (Deuteronomy 7:21, 10:17).

The Psalms also use this term as a synonym for God's awesomeness: "For *great* is the LORD and most worthy of praise; he is to be feared above all gods" (Psalm 96:4). Psalm 104, an account of God's rule over all His natural creation, begins with the exclamation, "O LORD my God, you are very *great*." In Psalm 150:2 we're commanded, "Praise him for his acts of power; praise him for his surpassing *greatness*."

Yet however great we may perceive God to be, we still have not fully grasped it: "*Great* is the LORD and most worthy of praise; his *greatness* no one can fathom" (Psalm 145:3). In a word, God's greatness is *infinite*.

"How great you are, O Sovereign LORD! There is no one like you, and there is no God but you." How awesome You are! How mighty and powerful You are! I glorify You as God and give thanks to You. You are worthy of all my praise forever. 2 Samuel 7:22; Romans 1:21; 1 Chronicles 16:25

Almighty and awesome God, reveal to me more and more of Your greatness, so that today and for all my days I may grow in fearing You and trusting You.

"I will exalt you, my God the King; I will praise your name for ever and ever." Psalm 145:1

And thank You, mighty Lord, for being just as much at work today on behalf of Your people as You were in Old Testament times. You have all the power necessary, and infinitely more, to accomplish everything You have planned for us and promised us. "My times are in your hands."

"Praise the LORD, O my soul. O LORD my God, you are very great." Romans 4:21; Psalms 31:15; 104:1

INFINITELY GREATER
THAN NATURE

One Old Testament passage especially emphasizes the greatness of God, and is thus designed to stimulate our fear of Him. Isaiah 40:12-31 contains a number of rhetorical questions and figures of speech describing God's immense greatness in creation and history. In doing so Isaiah uses several expressions that ascribe human characteristics to God. We see Him measuring with His hand, for example, though we know God doesn't have a physical body. Such anthropomorphic expressions are examples of how God condescends to reveal Himself in words we can understand.[9]

Isaiah's questioning begins: "Who has measured the waters in the hollow of his hand?" (verse 12). God is so great that all the waters of the seas could be measured, as it were, in the hollow of His hand. One day I borrowed one of my wife's measuring spoons to see how much water I could hold in the hollow of my hand. It was barely more than a tablespoonful.

By contrast, we know that slightly more than two-thirds of the earth's surface is covered with water, in places six miles deep. The total volume is incalculable. Even if we could estimate it in gallons (our largest unit of liquid measure), the number would be beyond our comprehension. Yet God says He holds all those waters in the hollow of His hand.

We see here the unfathomable distance between God and man—the infinitely vast chasm that yawns between Creator and creature. The dramatic contrast between the entire waters of the oceans and a mere tablespoonful in our hand shows us not just how small we are, but how great God is.

Next from Isaiah comes a second rhetorical question: "Who has...with the breadth of his hand marked off the heavens?" A handbreadth is the distance from the tip of the thumb to the tip of the little finger when the fingers are completely spread apart. This was a natural and universal measure of length in Bible times. Again to get an idea of what God is saying to us, I measured the breadth of my hand and found it to be just over eight inches.

God, by contrast, is so great that He marked off the heavens by the breadth of His hand. We can't really calculate the distance across the universe. We do know that the nearest star, other than the sun, is about four and a half light-years away. Since light travels at the speed of 186,000 miles per second, that nearest star is over twenty-six trillion miles away. Expressed numerically it looks like this:

26,000,000,000,000

And that's just to the nearest star! The distance across the entire universe, whatever it is, would simply be an incomprehensible figure to us. Yet God tells us He merely marks off that distance with the breadth of His hand.

The smallness of these two measures—the hollow and the breadth of the human hand—is intended to show us the immensity of God Himself, who can deal with the entire universe as we might deal with the most trivial objects. "And these are but the outer fringe of his works," we read in Job 26:14 about God's wonders in nature; "how faint the whisper we hear of him." When we've surveyed to our utmost all of creation, we've seen only the outer fringes of what God has done; we've heard only a whisper. Even the greatest conceivable measurements in creation are but an imperfect picture of how great God is. Truly our God is awesome. He is very great.

Isaiah continues: "Who has held the dust of the earth in a basket, or weighed the mountains on the scales and the hills in a balance?" The word translated "basket" is literally a "one-third measure," such as we might say "quart" to mean one-fourth of a gallon. It was undoubtedly a small amount. Yet God is so great He holds the dust of the earth in such a container and weighs the mountains on a set of scales.

I've visited Switzerland several times and am always awed by the rugged, majestic mountains there. Though I've never seen the Himalayas, I know they're higher and even more rugged and awesome. Whether it's the Alps or the Himalayas or our own Rocky Mountains, they always impress us with their grandeur and size. And yet God, as it were, weighs them on a balance scale.

Later in this chapter, Isaiah again draws our attention to creation:

> *Lift your eyes and look to the heavens:*
>   *Who created all these?*
> *He who brings out the starry host one by one,*
>   *and calls them each by name.*
> *Because of his great power and mighty strength,*
>   *not one of them is missing. (40:26)*

God created the stars, calls them each by name, and sustains them in their courses. One day on an airplane flight I found myself seated next to an astrophysicist. With this verse of Scripture in mind, I asked him how many stars are in the universe. His reply staggered me. He said there are about one hundred billion galaxies, each one containing about one hundred billion stars. A hundred billion times a hundred billion! Yet the Bible says, "He determines the number of the stars and calls them each by name" (Psalm 147:4).

There are just fewer than six billion people on the earth today, and many of us have the same names. Let's suppose, then, there are approximately three billion different names for people. Imagine trying to come up with that many. Yet God names a hundred billion times a hundred billion stars. We've given a few names to stars, constellations, and galaxies such as Polaris, Orion, or the Milky Way, but God names them all. Not only that, but because of His great power and mighty strength, not one of them is missing. They're part of the "all things" sustained by the powerful word of God the Son (Hebrews 1:3).

The oceans, the mountains, the heavens—all incalculable to us, but not to God. Their measurements are trivial to Him. The hollow of the hand, the breadth of the hand, and the balance scales all speak of easy competence in relation to the task. Isaiah says in effect, Consider the greatest things in nature—boundless seas, infinitely vast heavens, and majestic peaks. Though they are great, they are nothing in comparison to God.

As we think about these truths we will more and more appreciate God's greatness and grandeur and grow in our awe of Him.

Today, O Lord, I worship you with gladness. I exalt You as the One who owns and controls all the immeasurable universe. This wonderful earth is Yours, "and everything in it, the world and all who live in it." I worship You, O Lord, "the God of heaven, who

made the sea and the land." I worship You as the Master Designer of the day and night skies, "who brings out the starry host one by one, and calls them each by name." Psalms 100:2; 24:1; Jonah 1:9; Isaiah 40:26

"Let the heavens rejoice, let the earth be glad; let the sea resound, and all that is in it." "Let the rivers clap their hands, let the mountains sing together for joy." Psalms 96:11; 98:8

And yet all this vastness of all that You've created is as nothing in light of all that You really are. It is only a tiny glimpse of Your greatness, a whisper of Your awesomeness. In comparison to You, how small the universe is, and how small we are.

O Lord, my God, how great Thou art!

Praise be to You, O Lord. "From everlasting to everlasting you are God." "Yours, O LORD, is the greatness and the power and the glory and the majesty and the splendor, for everything in heaven and earth is yours. Yours, O LORD, is the kingdom; you are exalted as head over all. Wealth and honor come from you; you are the ruler of all things. In your hands are strength and power to exalt and give strength to all." Now, my God, I give You thanks, and praise Your glorious name. Psalm 90:2; 1 Chronicles 29:11-13

INFINITELY GREATER THAN THE NATIONS

As we continue in Isaiah 40, the prophet also shows us God's greatness as manifested in His superiority over the nations:

> *Surely the nations are like a drop in a bucket;*
> *they are regarded as dust on the scales;*
> *he weighs the islands as though they were fine dust.*
> *Lebanon is not sufficient for altar fires,*
> *nor its animals enough for burnt offerings.*
> *Before him all the nations are as nothing;*
> *they are regarded by him as worthless*
> *and less than nothing. (verses 15-17)*

Verse 15 begins with *surely,* an intensive word giving emphasis to what Isaiah is about to say. Other Bible translations have the word *behold* here as an imperative verb to get our attention. We might say, "Think of this!" Isaiah wants to arrest our attention; what he will tell us is so incredible that we need to stop and consider and ponder. And his message is this: Before God, the nations are no more than a drop in a bucket.

Think of that! The world's most powerful nations all totaled together are no more to God than a single drop in a bucket, or a drop of moisture falling from a bucket, as it has also been translated. A bucketful of water is something, but a drop is nothing. It is infinitesimal. Such are the nations before God.

The next comparison is even more incredible. God regards the nations as simply dust on the scales. The picture is of a pair of balance scales like we might use in a science laboratory, and which in Bible times were used in ordinary commerce. We know that any dust on the trays would be immaterial, having no effect on the accuracy of measurement.

Imagine buying fruit and vegetables at your local supermarket, then telling the clerk at the counter, "Please wipe the dust off the scales before weighing my produce—I don't want to pay for the dust." Such a concern is absurd. The weight of the dust is insignificant, irrelevant. And to God, the world's nations are nothing more than that.

It's not that the nations aren't imposing enough on a human level. Some of them down through history have been world empires. But however great they are or were, God is infinitely greater. Before Him all the most powerful states in all of history are no more than a drop in a bucket or dust on scales.

Another picture of the nations is brought before us in verse 16: "Lebanon is not sufficient for altar fires." Here the idea is not the power of the nations but their natural resources. Lebanon is singled out as an example. In Isaiah's day this land was noted for dense forests, and the "cedars of Lebanon" was a well-known expression. Psalm 92:12, for example, says, "The righteous…will grow like a cedar of Lebanon."

Solomon used cedars from Lebanon when he built God's temple in Jerusalem. Shifts of ten thousand men at a time were involved in cutting trees and hauling them to the sea where they were then floated on rafts to Israel's coast (see Kings 5:8-14). But Isaiah tells us that all the trees of Lebanon would not be sufficient for an altar fire worthy of the dignity and greatness of God.

In verse 17, Isaiah now strengthens the contrast between God and the power of the nations. The nations are seen "before" God—that is, in comparison with God—as "nothing," "worthless," and "less than nothing." Stronger language could not be used. *Nothing* means nonexistent, and *less than nothing* intensifies that idea. *Worthless* conveys the concept of being entirely empty of meaning or purpose.

Compared with God, the nations are only that. After all, He is the Creator who brought them into being and who entirely controls their existence: "From one man he made every nation of men, that they should inhabit the whole earth; and he determined the times set for them and the exact places where they should live" (Acts 17:26).

The purpose of these comparisons is not to disparage the nations, but rather to communicate how great God is. As with nature, Isaiah is saying, so it is with the nations: The sum of all their power is indeed great, but compared with God they are nothing and worthless. Let your mind soar to either the most exalted things in all of creation or the most powerful nations in all of history; when you have reached that point, consider that God is infinitely greater, without any limitation whatsoever.

No wonder the psalmist says, "His greatness no one can fathom" (Psalm 145:3). We can never comprehend Him, but only bow in awe and adoration before Him.

Isaiah goes on to emphasize that God is not only superior to the nations, but also sovereign over their rulers:

He brings princes to naught
  and reduces the rulers of this world to nothing.
No sooner are they planted,
  no sooner are they sown,
  no sooner do they take root in the ground,

than he blows on them and they wither,
    and a whirlwind sweeps them away like chaff.
        (40:23-24)

Not only the nations, but also their kings and emperors are reduced to nothingness before God, completely subject to His sovereign power. As Proverbs 21:1 says, "The king's heart is in the hand of the LORD; he directs it like a watercourse wherever he pleases." In our day of figurehead kings and queens, it may be difficult to appreciate what Solomon said. In his time the monarch was absolute. There was no legislature to pass laws he didn't like, no judicial court to restrain him. He was president, Congress, and the Supreme Court rolled into one. His authority was unconditional and unrestrained.

But the king's heart, Solomon says, is controlled by God. He directs the stubborn will of the most powerful monarch as easily as a farmer channels the flow of water in his irrigation canals.

God controls the destinies of rulers as well as their actions. They are scarcely in their place of authority before He "blows on them and they wither, and a whirlwind sweeps them away like chaff." Psalm 2 portrays the kings of the earth taking their stand against God, then says, "The One enthroned in heaven laughs; the Lord scoffs at them" (verse 4).

Think of the great rulers of history. Nebuchadnezzar, king of the Babylonian Empire, was driven insane in a moment and for seven years ate grass as cattle do, until God restored him. Alexander the Great conquered most of the known world, then died when he was only thirty-two. Napoleon and Hitler tried to conquer all of Europe, yet Napoleon died in exile and Hitler in a besieged bunker. Truly the most powerful rulers of all time have ultimately faded before the sovereign power of the One who rules history.

I praise you, O Most High. I honor and glorify You as the eternal God who lives forever. Your dominion is an eternal dominion; Your kingdom endures from generation to generation. You do as You please with the powers of heaven and the peoples and rulers of the earth, and ultimately no one has justification to doubt the wisdom of Your actions. Daniel 4:34-35

"Therefore I will praise you, O LORD, among the nations; I will sing praises to your name." 2 Samuel 22:50

I worship You as the Judge of all the earth. You are coming to judge the world in righteousness and the peoples in truth. And although as history progresses the nations in their pride and prosperity continue to "rage like the raging sea" and to "roar like the roaring of great waters," the day is coming when they will finally be still and know that You are God; You will be exalted among the nations, You will be exalted in the earth. Psalm 96:13; Isaiah 17:12; Psalm 46:10

I worship You, O God, "the blessed and only Ruler, the King of kings and Lord of lords," who in Your own time will bring about the appearing of our Lord Jesus Christ. 1 Timothy 6:15

Thank You for exalting Your Son, Jesus, to the highest place and giving Him the name that is above every name, that at His name every knee will bow, in heaven and on earth and under the earth, and every tongue confess that He is Lord. Philippians 2:9-11

"Amen. Come, Lord Jesus." Revelation 22:20

To You, O God my Father and the Father of our Lord Jesus Christ, "be the glory and the power for ever and ever. Amen." 1 Peter 4:11

"How awesome is the LORD Most High, the great King over all the earth!" Psalm 47:2

TO TRUST HIM MORE

Through word pictures of God's immensity, sovereignty, and power in Isaiah 40, the prophet is seeking to communicate to us something of the greatness of God. As the Westminster Shorter Catechism says, He is infinite, eternal, and unchangeable. His infinity means He is totally without limits. If the waters of the earth were twice as much as they actually are, He would still hold them in the hollow of His hand. If there were ten or a hundred times as many stars in the universe, He would still sustain them in their respective courses and call them each by name. If every nation of the world were to unite against Him, the One enthroned in heaven would still scoff at them; in His time and in His way He would blow on them and they would wither. Truly God's greatness no one can fathom.

What's the point of all this? The answer is found in Isaiah 40:18—"To whom, then, will you compare God?"—and again in verse 25, " 'To whom will you compare me? Or who is my equal?' says the Holy One." God wants us to see and understand that He is inconceivably great, that nothing or no one can possibly compare with Him.

The fact is, we do compare God to our circumstances, our problems, and the issues of society around us. We compare—and these circumstances and problems often seem bigger than God. Moses did this when the people of Israel grumbled over their lack of meat. God had promised to give them meat not for a day, but for a month until they loathed it. Moses was incredulous:

> *Here I am among six hundred thousand men on foot, and you say, "I will give them meat to eat for a whole month!" Would they have enough if flocks and herds were slaughtered for them? Would they have enough if all the fish in the sea were caught for them? (Numbers 11:21-22)*

Moses compared God to their situation—out in the desert with no visible source of meat—and found God wanting. At least for that moment Moses did not believe in God's infinite power, even after seeing the ten plagues in Egypt and experiencing the miraculous crossing of the Red Sea. Note God's answers to him:

> *Is the LORD's arm too short? You will now see whether or not what I say will come true for you. (11:23)*

"Is the LORD's arm too short?" This is obviously a rhetorical question. The answer is, of course not! God also asked Abraham's wife, Sarah, "Is anything too hard for the LORD?" (Genesis 18:14), and He said through the prophet Jeremiah, "I am the LORD, the God of all mankind. Is anything too hard for me?" (Jeremiah 32:27). Again the answer is an emphatic no. As the angel Gabriel told Mary, "Nothing is impossible with God" (Luke 1:37).

In Psalm 50:21, God says, "You thought I was altogether like you." One of our problems is that we tend to think God is like us—or perhaps like us, only more so. We have some power, but we know God has more. We have some wisdom, but God has more. We can handle some circumstances, but we hope God can handle more. We thus limit God to what we can imagine as possibilities.

Isaiah 40 reminds us that God is far, far greater than anything we can imagine. He is not limited to our most creative ideas. There can be no comparison between God—infinite, eternal, self-sufficient—and man, any man, for we are all only creatures, finite, limited, and mortal. If we're to "worship God acceptably with reverence and awe" (Hebrews 12:28), the infinitely vast distance between God and ourselves must ever be kept in mind. Isaiah 40 will help us keep this perspective.

Remember the response of the Israelites after crossing the Red Sea? After seeing the Lord's great power displayed, they feared the Lord and put their trust in Him. We, too, will trust God to the extent we fear Him; to the extent we stand in absolute awe and amazement at His great power and sovereign rule over all His creation. Frequent meditation on passages of Scripture such as Isaiah 40 will help us fear the Lord and be able to trust Him more.

Infinite God, eternal God, unchangeable God, I worship You in amazement.

With You, nothing is ever impossible. Luke 1:37

With You, there are never any limits. In all things, You are "able to do immeasurably more than all we ask or imagine." Ephesians 3:20

"From the rising of the sun to the place where it sets, the name of the LORD is to be praised." So I praise Your name today, heavenly Father. Psalm 113:3

And I trust in You. I put my hope in You. O God of hope, fill me with all joy and peace as I trust in You, so that I might overflow with hope by the power of Your Holy Spirit. "Guard my life, for I am devoted to you. You are my God." Romans 15:13; Psalm 86:2

An Awesomeness to Cherish

Everything about God is fitted to fill our minds with awe and supreme veneration. He is the inexhaustible fountain of all being, all life, all intelligence, all wisdom, all power, all good, and all true happiness in the universe.

He "gives all men life and breath and everything else" (Acts 17:25), and "every good and perfect gift" is from Him (James 1:17).

Reality is that "in him we live and move and have our being" (Acts 17:28); each of us can confess with David, "My times are in your hands" (Psalm 31:15).

He is "the blessed and only Ruler, the King of kings and Lord of lords, who alone is immortal and who lives in unapproachable light, whom no one has seen or can see" (1 Timothy 6:15-16).

He is "sovereign over the kingdoms of men and gives them to anyone he wishes and sets over them the lowliest of men" (Daniel 4:17).

It is He who judges: "He brings one down, he exalts another" (Psalm 75:7).

"For from him and through him and to him are all things. To him be the glory forever! Amen" (Romans 11:36).

Therefore, to fear God and to acceptably worship Him is to cherish an awesome sense of His greatness, grandeur, and excellence as these perfections are revealed to us both in His Word and in His works. Every time we look up into the sky, we should reflect on the fact that He measures those heavens by the breadth of His hand. Every time we see the ocean or even a lake, we can remember that He holds these waters in the hollow of His hand. Every time I drive out of our neighborhood and look at fourteen-thousand-foot Pikes Peak, I should remember that He weighs the mountains in a pair of balance scales.

We need both God's Word and His works to stimulate our fear of Him. The Bible interprets creation for us, and creation illustrates the Bible. David's Psalm 19 beautifully brings together these two aspects of God's revelation of Himself. The first part of the psalm declares God's revelation in nature, beginning with the well-known opening verse: "The heavens declare the glory of God; the skies proclaim the work of his hands."

In the center of the psalm, David extols God's revelation of Himself in His Word, beginning with another familiar expression: "The law of the LORD is perfect" (verse 7). Six different synonyms are used to describe the Word of God. It is called the law, the statutes, the precepts, the commands, the fear, and the ordinances of the Lord. "The fear of the LORD" (verse 9) is a strikingly unusual description of God's truth, emphasizing its effect on our hearts—through it, we learn to fear the Lord.

As we learn to see God in both His Word and His works, we'll begin to say with the prophet Jeremiah:

> *No one is like you, O LORD;*
>> *you are great,*
>> *and your name is mighty in power.*
> *Who should not revere you,*
>> *O King of the nations?*
>> *This is your due.*
> *Among all the wise men of the nations*
>> *and in all their kingdoms,*
>> *there is no one like you. (Jeremiah 10:6-7)*

But in all of our meditation on God's greatness and grandeur, we should remember that when we have strained our faculties to the utmost, we are still an immeasurable distance from the reality of who He is. He is truly an infinitely awesome God whom we should fear.

Awesome God, I worship You.

With the eyes of my heart I can see You "robed in splendor, striding forward in the greatness" of Your strength. With the ears of my heart I hear You say, "It is I, speaking in righteousness, mighty to save." Isaiah 63:1

I praise you, O Lord, and I testify, "Surely God is my salvation; I will trust and not be afraid. The LORD, the LORD, is my strength and my song; he has become my salvation." Isaiah 12:1-2

"O Sovereign LORD, you have begun to show to your servant your greatness and your strong hand." Upon Your awesome strength I lean and depend and rely. "You are a shield around me, O LORD." "You are my hiding place; you will protect me from trouble and surround me with songs of deliverance." "Surely God is my help; the Lord is the one who sustains me." Deuteronomy 3:24; Psalms 3:3; 32:7; 54:4

Lord God, infinite in power and might, "You are my God, and I will give you thanks; you are my God, and I will exalt you." Psalm 118:28

O glorious God! The vast oceans You hold in Your hand and the billions of stars You hold in their courses are but faint pictures of Your infinite greatness. Indeed You spoke the universe into existence in the beginning, and now by Your mighty power You hold it all together from hour to hour.

Fill our minds with awe and adoration as we think upon Your greatness. Fill our hearts with gratitude and gladness as we realize that with all Your infinite power and sovereignty, You have condescended to be our God.

Through Jesus Your Son we praise You.
Amen.

Part II

FOR YOUR HOLINESS, O GOD, I EXALT YOU

You are enthroned as the Holy One;
you are the praise of Israel.

PSALM 22:3

Worship the LORD in the splendor of his holiness;
tremble before him, all the earth.

PSALM 96:9

TOTALLY SET APART

One of the favorite hymns of the church is the grand and majestic "Holy, Holy, Holy." It seems to be equally appreciated both by people who prefer traditional hymns and by those who favor the contemporary choruses so popular today. "Holy, Holy, Holy" is often sung at conferences where I speak, and every time I hear it I get a tingling down my spine. Sometimes I'm so overcome with a sense of worship that I can't continue singing; I have to just stop and listen to other voices lifted in praise to God.

Why would this hymn capture such widespread appreciation and cause a great swelling of emotion in my own heart? It's because the writer (Reginald Heber) addresses the preeminent perfection of God—His holiness. Consider just these two stanzas:

Holy, holy, holy, Lord God Almighty!
Early in the morning our song shall rise to Thee;
Holy, holy, holy! Merciful and mighty!
God in three persons, blessed Trinity!

Holy, holy, holy! Though the darkness hide Thee,
Though the eye of sinful man Thy glory may not see;
Only Thou art holy—there is none beside Thee
Perfect in pow'r, in love and purity.

The threefold ascription "Holy, holy, holy" is taken from the classic passage on the holiness of God, Isaiah 6:1-8. There the prophet Isaiah sees God in His resplendent glory and hears the seraphs (meaning "burning ones") calling to one another, "Holy, holy, holy is the LORD Almighty; the whole earth is full of his glory."

The Hebrew language uses repetition to indicate emphasis, as we do by italics or underlining. Jesus frequently uses this device when He says, "Truly, truly" (as in John 3:3, NASB). To say something three times makes a statement even more emphatic. It expresses a superlative degree or indicates totality. By employing this threefold repetition for His holiness, God is exalting His holiness to the highest possible measure.

God is infinitely glorious in all His attributes, but only His holiness is magnified with this threefold ascription. We never read that He is "wise, wise, wise" or "powerful, powerful, powerful," but twice we hear the heavenly throne attendants calling out "Holy, holy, holy is the Lord God Almighty" (Isaiah 6:3; Revelation 4:8).

Why is God's holiness so exalted?

Edward J. Young says that holy, as used in Isaiah 6:3,

*signifies the entirety of the divine perfection which sepa-
rates God from His creation. God is the Creator who exists
in absolute independence of the creature. He is the Lord,
and not a man. Although the creation depends upon Him,
He Himself is entirely independent thereof.*[10]

So holiness represents "the entirety of the divine perfection," a perfection that sets Him totally apart from us.
Reading back through the hymn above, we notice the writer
encompasses the attributes of mercy, might, power, love,
and purity all within the meaning of God's holiness. The
holiness of God, in this respect, is not so much one of a
number of other attributes, but the sum of them all.

*This day, my song rises to Thee: "Holy, holy, holy, Lord God
Almighty.... Only Thou art holy—there is none beside Thee."*

*I praise You, Holy God, for Your divine and preeminent
perfection that sets You so totally apart from everything and
everyone else in all creation.*

*"The LORD is in his holy temple; the LORD is on his
heavenly throne."* Psalm 11:4

*I praise and thank You that Your grace and mercy are holy,
Your might and power are holy, Your love and faithfulness are
holy, Your justice and righteousness are holy, Your purity is
holy, Your wisdom is holy, and even Your wrath is holy.*

All that You are is holy, holy, holy. Therefore let all that I am praise You in this moment. "Praise the LORD, O my soul; all my inmost being, praise his holy name." Psalm 103:1

Loving Father, thank You for teaching us in Your Word about Your wonderful holiness. Teach me more and more to respond to Your holiness in the same way that the angels and saints do in the Scriptures. For You are eternally the Holy One, and "knowledge of the Holy One is understanding." Proverbs 9:10

GLORIOUS PERFECTION

The Puritan Stephen Charnock, in his classic book *The Existence and Attributes of God,* defined holiness as

> *a glorious perfection belonging to the nature of God. Hence he is in Scripture styled often the Holy One, the Holy One of Jacob, the Holy One of Israel; and oftener entitled Holy, than Almighty, and set forth by this part of his dignity more than any other.*[11]

Alec Motyer points out that "God's 'name' is qualified by the adjective 'holy' in the Old Testament more often than by all other qualifiers put together."[12]

The first and last songs of the Bible both magnify the holiness of God. Having crossed the Red Sea, Moses and the Israelites sang, "Who among the gods is like you, O LORD? Who is like you—*majestic in holiness,* awesome in glory, working wonders?" (Exodus 15:11). In Revelation 15:4 those who had been victorious over the beast sang, "Who will not fear you, O Lord, and bring glory to your name? For *you alone are holy.*" Note how both songs ascribe holiness to God alone. No creature in heaven or on earth, angelic or human, can share in God's holiness. He alone is holy.

The first petition Jesus told us to pray in the Lord's Prayer is "hallowed be your name." The word *hallow* means to make holy. Obviously we do not make God's name holy. Jesus is telling us to pray that God's name will be recognized and set apart as holy by people here on earth. If we take Jesus' sequence of petitions as indicative of priority, then recognizing God's holiness comes before even the coming of His kingdom or the doing of His will.

I still recall my first encounter with God's holiness, though it occurred almost forty years ago. I had received as a gift Charnock's *The Existence and Attributes of God.* Because I was deeply concerned about personal holiness, I turned immediately to the chapter on the holiness of God. I began reading and soon was driven to my knees before this holy God about whom I was learning. What Charnock wrote triggered in me a profound sense of the majesty and purity of God coupled with a painful awareness of my own creatureliness and sinfulness.

After a while I arose and began to read again. After a few more pages, I once more fell to my knees before Him, not as the result of a conscious decision but as a spontaneous response to what I was discovering about God's holiness. I was utterly in awe of God, and at the same time stricken with a sense of my own unworthiness before Him.

I don't want to suggest that Charnock's book will evoke a similar reaction from everyone. I think God simply used the book at that time to accomplish a particular work in my life. Perhaps it was my own micro-version of Isaiah's encounter with the holiness of God as recorded in Isaiah 6. In any event, since that time I've been captivated by His holiness. I've also learned that progress in personal holiness must be built upon an ever-deepening awareness of God's holiness.

"Our Father in heaven, hallowed be your name." May Your name be recognized and set apart as holy in my life today. Matthew 6:9

I praise You, Holy God, for Your beautiful and eternal perfection. "Holiness adorns your house for endless days, O LORD." Psalm 93:5

In Your Scriptures we read Your question, "'To whom will you compare me? Or who is my equal?' says the Holy One." The answer is that You, O Lord, are infinitely beyond compare! Isaiah 40:25

"Who is like you—majestic in holiness, awesome in glory?" Who is like You? No one is! Exodus 15:11

Only Thou art holy. "Who will not fear you, O Lord, and bring glory to your name? For you alone are holy." Yes, I glory in Your holy name as I come before You, and my heart rejoices. Revelation 15:4; 1 Chronicles 16:10

MORE THAN MORAL PURITY

When we think of God's holiness, the first thought that usually comes to mind is moral purity. This is certainly an important aspect of it, as we shall see. But when the seraphs called out "Holy, holy, holy," they meant something far more profound and fundamental.

The Hebrew word for holy is *qadosh,* which generally means "cut off" or "separate." When used of God, the word expresses the idea of separateness or "otherness." God is wholly "other" from all His creation, from angels, from people, and especially from sinful mankind. He is absolutely distinct from all His creatures and is infinitely exalted above them in incomprehensible glory and majesty. R. C. Sproul uses the word *transcendence* to describe this holiness:

> *When we speak of the transcendence of God we are talking about that sense in which God is above and beyond us. It tries to get at His supreme and altogether greatness....*

Transcendence describes God in His consuming majesty,
His exalted loftiness. It points to the infinite distance that
separates Him from every creature.[13]

An earlier writer, Arthur W. Pink, describes God as "solitary in His majesty, unique in His excellency, peerless in His perfections."[14]

In all I've read on God's holiness, I continually notice how authors search for words to adequately express the concept. Scan the three previous paragraphs and notice the superlative adjectives and adverbs: wholly, absolutely, infinitely, incomprehensible, supreme, consuming, exalted, solitary, unique, peerless. When we've exhausted the resources of our language, we still have not described God. He is indeed incomprehensible.

I like Sproul's choice of the word *transcendence*. Most other writers seem to choose *majesty* to denote God's holiness. Majesty refers to sovereign power, authority, or dignity. It speaks of grandeur and splendor. It can be a relative term, however, when we use it of human rulers—some are more sovereign or powerful than others; some have more grandeur and splendor. When we speak of God's majesty, we have to mean absolute, unequaled majesty. Since transcendence means over and above, I propose the expression *transcendent majesty* to enable us to come closest to an understanding of the holiness of God.

But perhaps when we've done all our explaining, we can't improve upon that threefold ascription of the seraphs who cried out, "Holy, holy, holy is the LORD Almighty." This is the heart response of all who fear God.

"Holy, holy, holy…Lord God Almighty." I praise You for Your incomprehensible glory, Your transcendent majesty. I praise You for being infinitely exalted above and beyond all mankind, above and beyond all angels, and above and beyond everything else in all creation. Revelation 4:8

"Praise the LORD, O my soul. O LORD my God, you are very great; you are clothed with splendor and majesty." Psalm 104:1

Upon Your throne You shine forth, "perfect in beauty." "You have set your glory above the heavens." Glorious God, "how majestic is your name in all the earth!" "O LORD, our LORD, how majestic is your name." Psalms 50:2; 8:1,9

"My mouth is filled with your praise, declaring your splendor all day long." Psalm 71:8

You have said, "I am the LORD; that is my name! I will not give my glory to another or my praise to idols." Therefore You have chosen "to bring low the pride of all glory and to humble all who are renowned on the earth." Yes, Holy God, You alone are worthy of all glory forever! Isaiah 42:8; 23:9

I worship You, and praise Your holy name. Psalm 30:4

LUSTER AND BRILLIANCE

Since God is holy, He is separate not only from His creation but also—in fact especially so—from sin. This leads us to the ethical aspect of God's holiness: the attribute of God commonly called His moral purity, the quality most popularly associated with the concept of His holiness.

We aren't wrong to think this way, since God Himself obviously had this dimension in mind when He said, "Be holy, because I am holy" (Leviticus 11:44-45; 1 Peter 1:16). Because of our creaturehood, we can never be like God in His transcendent majesty. But as people indwelt by His Holy Spirit, we should progressively become more like Him in His moral purity.

It would be wrong, however, to think of God's holiness exclusively in terms of moral purity. The majesty of God's holiness and its ethical aspects cannot be separated. They each give luster and brilliance to the other. The transcendent majesty of God gives weight to His moral purity. The ethical holiness of God gives beauty to His majesty.

Try to imagine a God who is infinite in His majesty, but not absolutely perfect in moral purity—with even just a fraction of a tendency toward abuse or contempt. Such a thought is terrifying. Stephen Charnock described this possibility well:

> *Though we conceive him infinite in majesty, infinite in essence, eternal in duration, mighty in power, and wise and immutable in his counsels,...yet if we conceive him destitute of this excellent perfection [of holiness], and imagine him possessed with the least contagion of evil, we make him but an infinite monster, and sully all those perfections we ascribed to him before.... It is a less injury to him to deny his being, than to deny the purity of it; the one makes him no god, the other a deformed, unlovely, and a detestable god.*[15]

Our Father in heaven, hallowed be Your name.

You have testified that You are zealous for Your holy name. You are entirely right to be this way, and therefore You are infinitely worthy of all my worship. For from You and through You and to You are all things. To You "be the glory forever! Amen." Ezekiel 39:25; Romans 11:36

In Your Word you say to me, "The LORD Almighty is the one you are to regard as holy, he is the one you are to fear, he is the one you are to dread." Yes, You alone are entirely pure and holy, and You alone are worthy of my total reverence and awe. Isaiah 8:13

I praise You that in Your complete holiness You are infinitely separate from any and all sin. "Your eyes are too pure to look on evil; you cannot tolerate wrong." "You are not a God who takes pleasure in evil; with you the wicked cannot dwell. The arrogant cannot stand in your presence; you hate all who do wrong. You destroy those who tell lies; bloodthirsty and deceitful men the LORD abhors." You indeed, O God, are "a consuming fire." Habakkuk 1:13; Psalm 5:4-6; Hebrews 12:29

"I will proclaim the name of the LORD. Oh, praise the greatness of our God!" You are "a faithful God who does no wrong, upright and just." Deuteronomy 32:3-4

Holy and awesome is Your name. Psalm 111:9

NO DARKNESS AT ALL

Thankfully, God is infinitely holy in His moral purity. "God is light," Scripture declares; "in him there is no darkness at all" (1 John 1:5). Light and darkness here have moral qualities standing for purity and impurity. John says there is no impurity at all in God. He is only and totally pure. A famous slogan for Ivory Soap is "ninety-nine and forty-four one-hundredths percent pure." Apparently that's quite an achievement for soap. To say, however, that God is 99.44 percent morally pure would be utter blasphemy. The only appropriate expression for God is *infinitely pure.*

Louis Berkhof points out that "the idea of ethical holiness is not merely negative (separation from sin); it also has a positive content, namely, that of moral excellence, or ethical perfection."[16] Alec Motyer gets at the same idea when he speaks of God's "total and unique moral majesty."[17] Once again we see writers searching for words adequate to express a concept beyond us.

Perhaps we can gain an idea of God's infinite moral perfection by going back to the comparisons we saw in

Isaiah 40. If a tablespoonful of water in the hollow of my hand represents my holiness, then the waters covering the earth represent God's. If the eight-inch breadth of my hand is a picture of my moral excellence, then the entire span of the universe is a picture of God's. Only by ascribing to it the same infiniteness that Isaiah attributes to His immensity and power can we do justice to the holiness of God.

Our Father in heaven, hallowed be Your name. I worship You today as I enter Your holy presence by the body and blood of Your Holy Son, Jesus Christ. Hebrews 10:19-20

"The LORD is in his holy temple." "And in his temple all cry, 'Glory!'" Psalms 11:4; 29:9

"Glory to God in the highest." "Be exalted, O God, above the heavens, and let your glory be over all the earth." Luke 2:14; Psalm 108:5

"Your ways, O God, are holy." Father of light, in whom "there is no darkness at all," I praise You for Your infinite holiness. You live "in unapproachable light, whom no one has seen or can see." Psalm 77:13; James 1:17; 1 John 1:5; 1 Timothy 6:16

Thank You, Father of light, for sending into my life "the light of the world"—Your Son, Jesus, who is "the true light that gives light to every man." "You, O LORD, keep my lamp burning; my God turns my darkness into light." John 8:12; 1:9; Psalm 18:28

"In your light we see light." Loving Father, thank You for the light You give to me through the Bible and through Your Holy Spirit. "Your word is a lamp to my feet and a light for my path." Your commands "are radiant, giving light to the eyes." Because You are holy, Your words "are flawless, like silver refined in a furnace of clay, purified seven times." And in Your Word I see this wonderful promise: "The LORD will be your everlasting light, and your God will be your glory." Psalm 36:9; 119:105; 19:8; 12:6; Isaiah 60:19

Thank You, my God and Father, my Light and my Glory! You, O Lord, are my Holy One, my Creator, and my King. Isaiah 43:15

THE ONLY
APPROPRIATE
RESPONSE

As indicated earlier, Isaiah 6:1-8 is universally recognized as the classic passage on God's holiness. All the books I've read on the subject, without exception, refer to it in some degree, and I can't recall ever hearing a sermon on the topic that didn't use it as a primary text.

What makes Isaiah 6 so important to worship is that it sets forth both the holiness of God and our only appropriate response to it. We see not only God's holiness magnified by the threefold call of the seraphs, "Holy, holy, holy," but also Isaiah's deep humiliation in his cry, "Woe to me! I am ruined!"

For your convenience I include the passage here in its entirety. If you're already familiar with it, I urge you to read it once again, slowly and prayerfully, to fully appreciate Isaiah's encounter with the holiness of God.

*In the year that King Uzziah died, I saw the Lord seated
on a throne, high and exalted, and the train of his robe
filled the temple. Above him were seraphs, each with six
wings: With two wings they covered their faces, with two
they covered their feet, and with two they were flying. And
they were calling to one another:*

*"Holy, holy, holy is the LORD Almighty;
the whole earth is full of his glory."*

*At the sound of their voices the doorposts and thresholds
shook and the temple was filled with smoke.*

*"Woe to me!" I cried. "I am ruined! For I am a
man of unclean lips, and I live among a people of unclean
lips, and my eyes have seen the King, the LORD Almighty."*

*Then one of the seraphs flew to me with a live coal in his
hand, which he had taken with tongs from the altar. With it
he touched my mouth and said, "See, this has touched your
lips; your guilt is taken away and your sin atoned for."*

*Then I heard the voice of the Lord saying, "Whom
shall I send? And who will go for us?"*

And I said, "Here am I. Send me!" (Isaiah 6:1-8)

One of the first questions coming to mind from this
passage might be this: Which aspect of God's holiness is in

view here? Is it His transcendent majesty or His moral purity? The answer is both.

The vision of God seated on a throne, high and exalted, with the train of His robe filling the temple, is an inescapable picture of His majesty. The words *throne, high,* and *exalted* first draw our attention to this aspect. The train of His robe filling the temple deepens our impression of His supreme royalty. The sinless seraphs covering their faces before Him are a sign of reverence and awe before this unspeakably exalted One, as they cry, "Holy, holy, holy."

It was not just God's transcendent majesty, however, that caused Isaiah's deep cry of dismay. It was also the awareness of His blazing moral purity, revealing as it did Isaiah's own sinfulness. H. H. Rowley gives this reason for the prophet's response: "It is not the consciousness of humanity in the presence of divine power, but the consciousness of sin in the presence of moral purity."[18]

So it is with us: Our reaction to God's majestic holiness is a realization of our own insignificance; our response to His ethical holiness is an awareness of our sinfulness and impurity.

The seraphs, having sinless natures, see the holiness of God and react to it with awe and adoration. Isaiah experiences the same thing, but feels it as a sinner. That is the reason he cries out in woe and ruin.

Isaiah was a righteous man, in fact a prophet of God. Yet he now describes himself as "a man of unclean lips." Seeing God in His holiness, Isaiah views himself as morally impure. His own holiness has suddenly become to him no more than a tablespoonful of water in the hollow of his hand.

This word *unclean* is significant. It's the word that was to be uttered by lepers who, as they walked along, must cry out "Unclean! Unclean!" (Leviticus 13:45). Isaiah uses it again in Isaiah 64:6 when he says, "All of us have become like one who is *unclean,* and all our righteous acts are like filthy rags." Now in this encounter with the holiness of God, Isaiah uses it of himself. If leprosy typified sin, then Isaiah saw his sinfulness as moral leprosy.

Father in heaven, hallowed be Your name.

"You are enthroned as the Holy One; you are the praise of Israel." You formed Your people for Yourself that they may proclaim Your praise. Therefore I worship and praise You. "Great is the Holy One of Israel." Psalm 22:3; Isaiah 43:21; 12:6

"The LORD is in his holy temple." "Exalt the LORD our God and worship at his footstool; he is holy." Yes, "exalt the LORD our God and worship at his holy mountain, for the LORD our God is holy." Habakkuk 2:20; Psalm 99:5,9

"My mouth will speak in praise of the LORD. Let every creature praise his holy name for ever and ever." Psalm 145:21

Almighty God, as I praise Your holiness, Your blazing moral purity, I cannot help being aware of my own sinfulness and impurity. Holy Father, I ask for Your help and power in my pursuit of holiness, for only by Your help can I make progress in obeying Your command to be holy as You are holy. "Look down from heaven and see from your lofty throne, holy and glorious." "I am poor and needy; come quickly to me, O God." 1 Peter 1:16; Isaiah 63:15; Psalm 70:5

HOLY JUSTICE, HOLY MERCY

Isaiah was completely devastated. He was disintegrated. If we left him at this point in Isaiah 6:5 there would be no hope for him or for us. But God does not leave Isaiah devastated. The Scripture (verse 6) tells us that one of the seraphs flew with a live coal from the altar and touched it to Isaiah's mouth.

"See," said the seraph, "this has touched your lips; your guilt is taken away and your sin atoned for." Think of the impact of those words upon Isaiah. Here was a prophet, a righteous man, who had just seen how unholy, how morally unclean he really was when confronted with the holiness of God. He had been shattered; he had declared moral bankruptcy. How could he possibly continue as a prophet after becoming so painfully aware of his own sinfulness?

Note that it is his lips Isaiah saw as unclean. Why not his hands or especially his heart? I believe it was because Isaiah's lips were his professional instruments. He spoke on behalf of God. Now Isaiah suddenly realizes that the very instruments he had been using for God are unclean. This would be like a surgeon ready to begin a delicate surgery only to discover that his hands were filthy—except that Isaiah could not scrub his lips as the surgeon can his hands.

But there *is* someone who can cleanse Isaiah's lips. It is God, who addresses Isaiah through the seraph: "Your guilt is taken away and your sin atoned for." How could God say this to Isaiah? Can God just arbitrarily forgive sin? Can He grant a pardon without full satisfaction of His justice?

The answer is no. God cannot subvert His justice any more than He can sin. God cannot magnify mercy at the expense of justice. We tend to think of justice in a positive sense—as something that is on our side. A child is murdered in the community and everyone wants to "see justice done." We want the perpetrator tried, convicted, and sentenced to severe punishment. That would be justice in our minds. But the murderer doesn't want justice. If tried and found guilty, he hopes for leniency, not justice. He doesn't want to receive what he deserves. He wants mercy.

Suppose the judge in such a case is overly lenient and pronounces a light sentence. What would be the community's response? There would be a tremendous cry of outrage. People would feel justice had been violated, that the guilty person did not receive the punishment justice required.

In our initial standing before God as guilty sinners, justice is not on our side. It's against us. The sentence has already been handed down. The wages of sin is death. In this case we don't want to "see justice done." We want mercy. But God's justice is a holy justice; a perfect justice. God cannot be lenient like the judge. He cannot violate His own justice.

What is the solution? Isaiah himself would later give us the answer in the beautiful prophecy of chapter 53. The prophet's filthy lips, now cleansed by God, would utter those immortal words: "We all, like sheep, have gone astray, each of us has turned to his own way; *and the LORD has laid on him the iniquity of us all*" (53:6). Isaiah prophesied of One who would satisfy God's justice against us by Himself bearing the awful punishment we deserve.

That's why God could say to Isaiah, "Your guilt is taken away and your sin atoned for." According to God's plan, some seven hundred years later His own Son would pay for Isaiah's guilt and satisfy His justice. Jesus Christ reconciled God's justice and His mercy.

Holy Father, I come now before You to worship You. "Exalted be God my Savior!" Psalm 18:46

Thank You for making known to Your people and to all the world both Your holy justice and Your holy mercy.

I praise You for Your justice and Your righteousness. "Your righteousness is like the mighty mountains, your justice like the great deep." Your Word tells me, "The LORD is righteous, he loves justice." You are indeed "a righteous judge, a God who expresses his wrath every day." "Your wrath is as great as the fear that is due you"—and the fear that is due You is infinite. Psalms 36:6; 11:7; 7:11; 90:11

I praise You for the righteousness and holiness of Your Son, Jesus, "whose eyes are like blazing fire" and who bears "the sharp, double-edged sword." Like Simon Peter in Galilee long ago, I have come to "believe and know" that Jesus is indeed "the Holy One of God." Revelation 2:18; 2:12; John 6:69

Almighty Father, I also praise and thank You for Your holy mercy, Your "tender mercy," Your "great mercy" by which You have saved me and given me new birth. You are "full of compassion and mercy." Therefore I approach Your throne of grace with confidence, so that I may receive mercy and find grace to help in my time of need. Luke 1:78; 1 Peter 1:3; Titus 3:5; James 5:11; Hebrews 4:16

Thank You for the amazing truth that by Your mercy, as well as by Your fatherly discipline, I can actually come to share in Your holiness. I "have been made holy through the sacrifice of the body of Jesus Christ once for all." You chose me in Christ "before the creation of the world to be holy and blameless" in Your sight. Hebrews 12:10; 10:10; Ephesians 1:4

You have done great things for me, and I am filled with joy. Psalm 126:3

"I will praise you, O LORD, with all my heart." Psalm 138:1

HIS HOLINESS AND MINE

How should we respond to the holiness of God?

Above all we should fear Him. In fact, like Jesus Himself (in the messianic prophecy of Isaiah 11:1-3), we should *delight* to fear God, learning to stand in reverential awe before His transcendent majesty and moral purity. We must learn to cultivate such an exalted view of God so that we fear Him as we ought.

We must do more, however. The fear of God should work its way out in our lives in the vigorous pursuit of holiness. As Paul says, "Let us cleanse ourselves from all defilement of flesh and spirit, *perfecting holiness in the fear of God*" (2 Corinthians 7:1, NASB). We are to be holy because He is holy (1 Peter 1:16).

The basic meaning of *holy* as "separate" applies to us as well as to God. Of course God *is* holy; He *is* separate from all moral impurity. We are not holy, but we can and must take steps to pursue holiness, to separate ourselves from sinful habits and practices.

Because God is holy, we also need to practice humility. God is infinite in His transcendent majesty and perfect in His moral purity. By contrast we are dependent, responsible but sinful creatures. On this earth we aren't likely to have a sudden overwhelming encounter with the holiness of God as Isaiah did, but God is no less holy today than He was when Isaiah saw Him in the temple. Deep humility is the only proper response as we see our sin in the light of His holiness.

Nothing produces humility in a Christian as much as an abiding sense of one's own sinfulness. For learning "genuine humility and self-abasement," John Calvin taught that we should be "empty of all opinion of our own virtue, and shorn of all assurance of our own righteousness—in fact, broken and crushed by the awareness of our own utter poverty."[19] As we seriously pursue holiness we'll grow in humility, for we discover, as Calvin said, that "our nature, wicked and deformed, is always opposing his uprightness; and our capacity, weak and feeble to do good, lies far from his perfection."[20]

Consider God's encouragement to those who seek humility:

For this is what the high and lofty One says—
he who lives forever, whose name is holy:

"I live in a high and holy place,
  but also with him who is contrite and lowly in spirit,
to revive the spirit of the lowly
  and to revive the heart of the contrite." (Isaiah 57:15)

This is an incredible promise. The high and lofty and holy God condescends to dwell with those who are humble, who are of a contrite and lowly spirit because of their sin. Surely this is worth the price of being "shorn of all assurance of our own righteousness" in order to learn humility.

In the splendor of Your holiness I worship You, O God Most High. You live forever, Your name is holy, and You dwell in a high and holy place. Psalm 29:2; Isaiah 57:15

"How lovely is your dwelling place, O LORD Almighty!" "You are awesome, O God, in your sanctuary." Yes, how infinitely high and lofty You are in heaven. Yet You promise to come down and dwell in the heart of one "who is contrite and lowly in spirit." This is the humble person who can say to You, "You stoop down to make me great." Psalms 84:1; 68:35; Isaiah 57:15; Psalm 18:35

Lord, Your Word reminds me that I am only dust, only a vanishing mist. In humility I acknowledge that this is true. So I ask You, "Part your heavens, O LORD, and come

down.... Reach down your hand from on high." Come
down and deliver me in this moment from any pride,
from any coldness toward You, and from any treasured
sin. ^{Psalm 103:14; James 4:14; Psalm 144:5,7}

"Send forth your light and your truth, let them guide me; let
them bring me to your holy mountain, to the place where you
dwell." I approach Your altar to encounter You, O God, "my joy
and my delight." "I will praise you…O God, my God." ^{Psalm 43:3-4}

"Blessed are those who dwell in your house; they are ever
praising you." Let me share in that blessing today. ^{Psalm 84:4}

In Your Word, I read Your promise: "I will show my
greatness and my holiness, and I will make myself known in
the sight of many nations." You have promised a coming day
when "men will look to their Maker and turn their eyes to
the Holy One of Israel." You have promised, "The LORD
will lay bare his holy arm in the sight of all the nations."
You have promised that "once more the humble will rejoice
in the LORD; the needy will rejoice in the Holy One of
Israel." You have promised that Your people "will keep my
name holy; they will acknowledge the holiness of the
Holy One of Jacob, and will stand in awe of the God of
Israel." ^{Ezekiel 38:23; Isaiah 17:7; 52:10; 29:19; 29:23}

O faithful God, I believe and eagerly await Your
fulfillment of all these promises. How I look forward to the
glorious day, when we will shout, "Hallelujah! For our Lord
God Almighty reigns." ^{Revelation 19:6}

While I wait for that day, I ask You to keep giving me Your strength and guidance and wisdom to daily pursue holiness, for You "did not call us to be impure, but to live a holy life." Help me heed Your good command to purify myself "from everything that contaminates body and spirit, perfecting holiness out of reverence for God." 1 Thessalonians 4:7; 2 Corinthians 7:1

And I will praise You and glorify You with thanksgiving. Psalm 69:30

ONLY BY HIS BLOOD

In responding to God's holiness, we'll also want to grow in gratitude to God for His mercy to us through Christ. We continually sin against His perfect moral purity, and our sin is aggravated by the greatness of His transcendent majesty. Each of us has committed high treason against the supreme, exalted Ruler of the universe—and we've done it again and again and again.

Yet God has not dealt with us in perfect justice as He could have. Rather He has extended mercy to us at the cost of His own dear Son. Surely such grace calls forth our deepest heartfelt gratitude. As those who have been forgiven much, we should love much (Luke 7:47).

Now we may enter into His presence with adoring reverence. In Old Testament times God dwelt symbolically in the Most Holy Place of the tabernacle or temple. Only the high priest was allowed to enter there, and then only once a year, and never without the blood of atonement. God demonstrated His holiness by maintaining this separation from the sinful people.

But all that has changed. When Jesus died on the cross, the temple curtain barring the way into the Most Holy Place was torn in two from top to bottom. Jesus opened the way of access for sinners to come into God's holy presence. In fact He invites us to come. We're all invited (not just the high priest), and we may come continually (not just once a year). "Therefore, brothers," says the writer of Hebrews, "since we have confidence to enter the Most Holy Place by the blood of Jesus…let us draw near to God with a sincere heart in full assurance of faith" (10:19,22).

One thing hasn't changed, however—the necessity of blood. In Old Testament times it was the blood of the sacrificial animal; now it is the blood of Jesus. We can come boldly and continually, but we must always come through the blood of Christ. Only He provides entry for sinners into fellowship with a holy God.

Had sin never entered the world, it still would be fitting for us to bow in reverential awe before Him. We would gladly join the seraphs in calling out, "Holy, holy, holy is the LORD Almighty; the whole earth is full of his glory."

But sin did enter the world—and because of His holiness, God now reveals Himself as the hater of sin and the just punisher of sinners. But He also reveals Himself in the person of His Son as a merciful and gracious Savior. Our awe of His holiness can be joined with amazement at His love.

Reflect on these words from John Brown, a nineteenth-century Scottish pastor and theologian:

Nothing is so well fitted to put the fear of God, which will preserve men from offending him, into the heart, as an enlightened view of the cross of Christ. There shine spotless holiness, inflexible justice, incomprehensible wisdom, omnipotent power, holy love. None of these excellencies darken or eclipse the other, but every one of them rather gives a lustre to the rest. They mingle their beams, and shine with united eternal splendour: the just Judge, the merciful Father, the wise Governor. Nowhere does justice appear so awful, mercy so amiable, or wisdom so profound.[21]

"I will give thanks to the LORD because of his righteousness and will sing praise to the name of the LORD Most High." Psalm 7:17

I praise You, Lord Most High, for Your infinite holiness. As I better understand it, I must thank You all the more for Your unexplainable mercy to me. I have continually sinned against Your perfect moral purity, and my sin is aggravated by the greatness of Your transcendent majesty. I have committed high treason against You, the supreme, exalted Ruler of the universe. I have done this again and again and again.

And yet You have shown me mercy! You have not treated me as my sins deserve or repaid me according to my iniquities.

You are "rich in mercy," and in Christ, through His blood,
You have lavished upon me the riches of Your amazing
grace. Thank You, loving Father! "The Lord our God is
merciful and forgiving, even though we have rebelled against
him." Psalm 103:10; Ephesians 2:4; 1:7-8; Daniel 9:9

Now by the blood of Jesus, my "merciful and faithful
high priest," I have confidence to enter Your Most Holy
Place. Therefore by His precious blood I now draw near to
You, O God, "with a sincere heart in full assurance of
faith." Hebrews 10:19; 2:17; 10:22

Lord Jesus, I give praise to You as my Holy Savior and the
perfect High Priest who meets my deepest need. You indeed
are "holy, blameless, pure, set apart from sinners, exalted above
the heavens." Hebrews 7:26

I have been redeemed from an empty life "not with
perishable things such as silver or gold," but with Your own
precious blood, Lord Jesus! You are the Lamb without blemish
or defect! You are the Lamb of God who takes away my sins!
Thank You, Holy Jesus. 1 Peter 1:18-19; John 1:29

"My mouth will speak in praise of the LORD. Let every
creature praise his holy name for ever and ever." Psalm 145:21

O holy God! The sinless seraphs covered their faces in Your presence. How much more should we who are but sinful creatures bow in reverence before Your throne. You alone are holy. You alone are the transcendent, majestic God. You alone are morally pure.

You are perfect light; in You there is no darkness at all. And yet, through Your Son You came to us as our Savior. You came not to pronounce woe but blessing to those who trust in Jesus. Fill our hearts with awe because of Your holiness and with amazement because of Your love.

Through Jesus Christ our Lord we praise You.
Amen.

Part III

FOR YOUR WISDOM, O GOD, I EXALT YOU

Oh, the depth of the riches of the wisdom and knowledge of God!
How unsearchable his judgments,
and his paths beyond tracing out!

ROMANS 11:33

His works are perfect.

DEUTERONOMY 32:4

Do you not know? Have you not heard?
Has it not been told you from the beginning?

ISAIAH 40:21

HIS WISDOM ON DISPLAY

During my brief stint as an engineer in the aircraft industry I observed two important truths that weren't stressed in school. First, I learned that the design of a jet airplane is very much a team effort. We had aeronautical, mechanical, electrical, and structural engineers all involved. Some engineers designed, others tested the designs, and still others purchased components from outside suppliers. It was a massive team effort. No one engineer could possibly design a jet airplane.

The second thing I came to realize is that much of engineering design is accomplished by trial and error. Using all their expertise, aeronautical engineers design an airfoil, test it in the wind tunnel, then modify it, test it, and modify it again. Or a computer circuit board is designed, only to discover that it, too, isn't quite right and must be changed, retested, and remodified. The process goes on, again and again. No component, regardless of how insignificant it seems, can be accepted when its design is only "almost right."

I came along as a young engineer at the time our company was building its first jet fighter. We created two prototypes and sent them to the air force for a long series of test flights. To the company's dismay the planes failed to perform according to air force specifications. It was back to the drawing board to redesign both fuselage and wings to increase the aircraft's speed and maneuverability. Finally the plane met the requirements and served the air force well for a number of years. But it took a lot of trial-and-error work to get it right.

Teamwork and trial and error—both are required to build a sophisticated jet fighter. But a fighter plane, complicated as it is, is simple compared to the human body. "Numberless are the world's wonders," said the ancient philosopher Sophocles, "but none more wondrous than the body of man."[22]

Consider just the heart. Think what a challenge it would be for a team of engineers to design a pump with these specifications:

- 75-year life expectancy (2.5 billion cycles)
- Requiring no maintenance or lubrication
- Output varying between .025 horsepower and short bursts of 1 horsepower
- Weight not exceeding 10.5 ounces (300 grams)

- Capacity of 2,000 gallons per day
- Valves operating 4,000 to 5,000 times per hour[23]

Or what structural engineer would want to tackle the design of the twenty-six bones of the human foot which, in the case of a soccer player, absorb a cumulative force of over one thousand tons in a single game?[24]

I admit to a fascination with the design of the human body. Though I'm not a scientist, I remember enough of my engineering studies to appreciate all I read about the incredible complexity and ingenious design of our bodies. I referred earlier to Michael Denton's book *Evolution: A Theory in Crisis.* To help us better understand the "unparalleled complexity and adaptive design" of a single human cell, Dr. Denton suggests we imagine magnifying it "a thousand million times until it is twenty kilometers in diameter and resembles a giant airship large enough to cover a great city like London or New York." On its surface we see what appear to be millions of portholes, opening and closing to allow a continual stream of materials flowing in and out. Entering one of these openings, we discover "a world of supreme technology and bewildering complexity":

We would see endless highly organized corridors and conduits branching in every direction away from the

> *perimeter of the cell, some leading to the central memory*
> *bank in the nucleus and others to assembly plants and pro-*
> *cessing units.... A huge range of products and raw*
> *materials would shuttle along all the manifold conduits in*
> *a highly ordered fashion to and from all the various assem-*
> *bly plants in the outer regions of the cell.*

"We would wonder," Dr. Denton continues, "at the level of control implicit in the movement of so many objects down so many seemingly endless conduits, all in perfect unison."

It would resemble "an immense automated factory, a factory larger than a city and carrying out almost as many unique functions as all the manufacturing activities of man on earth." In one respect, however, it would differ radically from the most advanced factory or machine known to man—"for it would be capable of replicating its entire structure within a matter of a few hours."[25]

Now consider that there are an estimated 75 trillion of these incredibly sophisticated cells in your body—75 trillion unique representations of this "object of unparalleled complexity and adaptive design." What keeps them all working together? It's the DNA strand locked away inside the nucleus of each cell. Your body's DNA is estimated to contain instructions that, if written out, would fill a thousand six-hundred-page books, yet all of it would fit inside an ice cube.[26]

However, "in terms of complexity," Dr. Denton adds, "an individual cell is nothing when compared with a system like the mammalian brain."

The human brain consists of about ten thousand million nerve cells. Each nerve cell puts out somewhere in the region of between ten thousand and one hundred thousand connecting fibers by which it makes contact with other nerve cells in the brain....

Despite the enormity of the number of connections, the ramifying forest of fibers is not a chaotic random tangle but a highly organized network in which a high proportion of the fibers are unique adaptive communication channels following their own specially ordained pathway through the brain. Even if only one hundredth of the connections in the brain were specifically organized, this would still represent a system containing a much greater number of specific connections than in the entire communications network on earth.[27]

What does all this fascinating information about the human body have to do with fearing and worshiping God? It's simply one illustration of thousands that could be drawn from nature's vast resources to demonstrate God's infinite wisdom, further motivating our praise.

Loving and wise Father, cause Your Holy Spirit to enable me now to worship You in a worthy manner, in a way that pleases You, "in spirit and in truth." John 4:24

In spirit and in truth, I praise You today for Your infinite wisdom displayed in the amazing complexity of every human body. "I praise you because I am fearfully and wonderfully made." Psalm 139:14

"Your works are wonderful, I know that full well." How true this is of all that You have made and all that You have done! As Your Word tells us, You made the earth by Your power, You founded the world by Your wisdom, You stretched out the heavens by Your understanding. Everything in all creation is like a miracle. "You are the God who performs miracles; you display your power among the peoples." Psalm 139:14; Jeremiah 51:15; Psalm 77:14-15

"Who is like you…working wonders?" No one is! "For you are great and do marvelous deeds; you alone are God." Exodus 15:11; Psalm 86:10-11

"Praise be to the LORD God…who alone does marvelous deeds." Psalm 72:18

SKILL AND JUDGMENT TO ADMIRE

By coming to appreciate and admire God's incomprehensible wisdom and skill, we can grow in reverential awe of Him.

Wisdom, as it pertains to us, is commonly defined as good judgment or the ability to develop the best course of action in response to a given situation. Our human wisdom is always exercised in the context of the situation in which we find ourselves. Even in initiating some new course of action we never start with a "clean sheet of paper." Whatever we plan is always affected by surrounding circumstances.

God did start with a clean sheet of paper. There were no external circumstances to affect His plans. He was free to do whatever He desired with His creation. How then can we define wisdom in that context?

Nineteenth-century theologian J. L. Dagg described God's wisdom as "consisting in the selection of the best end of action, and the adoption of the best means for the accomplishment of this end."[28] The best possible end of all God's actions is His own glory. Everything God does or allows in all His creation must ultimately serve His glory. There is no end higher than that because there's nothing or no one higher than God. "For from him and through him and to him are all things. To him be the glory forever! Amen" (Romans 11:36).

The concept of God's glory embraces much mystery that we cannot fully comprehend. We do know, however, that it includes the exaltation of His person and the display of all His splendor and wondrous perfections, including the perfection of His wisdom as we discover it in His creation, in His providence, and in His redemption of lost men and women.

How wise You are, O God! In Your perfect freedom, You have always chosen the best goal—Your own glory—in everything You do. And to accomplish that goal, You have always followed the best means in everything You do. "You, O LORD, are exalted forever." Psalm 92:8

Thank You, Father, for how You have displayed Your splendor and Your wonderful perfection in all You do and in all You are and think. "You make me glad by your deeds, O LORD; I sing for joy at the works of your hands. How great are your works, O LORD, how profound your thoughts!" Psalm 92:4-5

"O great and powerful God, whose name is the LORD Almighty, great are your purposes and mighty are your deeds." Yes, O Lord, "I stand in awe of your deeds." Jeremiah 32:18-19; Habakkuk 3:2

And I bring before You this desire: In all that I am and all that I do and all that I think, I want to glorify You. I look to You, Gracious Father, to work in my life and enable me to do this more and more.

"Be exalted, O God, above the heavens; let your glory be over all the earth." Psalm 57:5

"May the glory of the LORD endure forever; may the LORD rejoice in his works." Psalm 104:31

"To the only wise God be glory forever through Jesus Christ! Amen." Romans 16:27

HOW MANY INDEED!

The psalmist said, "How many are your works, O LORD! In wisdom you made them all; the earth is full of your creatures" (Psalm 104:24). All creation is like an art gallery in which God displays the splendor of His wisdom, and Psalm 104 is like a directory to it. I encourage you to walk leisurely through this psalm, pausing at each display of God's workmanship to admire and worship Him.

Then take time to gaze upon the wonderful works of nature as you see them in real life. Consider the beauty and fragrance of the flowers, the exquisite nature of the butterfly, the stateliness of the horse, the cuddliness of the little puppy. Look up at the stars in their courses and at the sun sending forth its life-giving rays. In all the works of nature let your mind dwell upon the glorious wisdom of God.

Not only do we see God's wisdom in the intricate designs of nature, but also in their endless variety. There are, for example, seven hundred varieties of butterflies and eight thousand varieties of moths in the United States and

Canada alone. How many indeed are Your works, O Lord! In commenting on that statement in Psalm 104:24, C. H. Spurgeon teaches us about the meaning behind it: "If the number of the creatures be so exceedingly great, how great, nay, immense, must needs be the power and wisdom of him who formed them all." Spurgeon considers how a craftsman who could produce not only clocks and watches but also pumps and mills and firearms would certainly be considered more skilled than if he could make only one of those types of products. Likewise Almighty God displays more wisdom "in forming such a vast multitude of different sorts of creatures, and all with admirable and irreprovable art, than if he had created but a few; for this declares the greatness and unbounded capacity of his understanding."[29]

What is more, in all of His creation God did not need a team of engineers to do His design work. God simply spoke, and all the teeming works of nature came into being. Their various designs existed in His infinite mind from all eternity.

Nor did God have to rely on trial and error as we do. "God saw that it was good" is a continual refrain throughout the Genesis 1 account of creation. Even the most skilled craftsman, when he has finished a piece of work, can find some minute flaw in it, but "God saw all that he had made, and it was *very* good" (Genesis 1:31).

Mighty God, Creator of all things in all their variety, I worship You. And in this quiet moment of worship, by Your amazing provision of prayer I call upon all that You have created to join with me in worship.

"Praise the LORD. Praise the LORD from the heavens, praise him in the heights above. Praise him, all his angels, praise him, all his heavenly hosts. Praise him, sun and moon, praise him, all you shining stars.... Praise the LORD from the earth, you great sea creatures and all ocean depths, lightning and hail, snow and clouds, stormy winds that do his bidding, you mountains and all hills, fruit trees and all cedars, wild animals and all cattle, small creatures and flying birds, kings of the earth and all nations, you princes and all rulers on earth, young men and maidens, old men and children. Let them praise the name of the LORD, for his name alone is exalted; his splendor is above the earth and the heavens." Psalm 148:1-3, 7-13*

"Praise the LORD, all his works everywhere in his dominion." Psalm 103:22*

"Praise the LORD, O my soul." Psalm 103:1*

Thank You, God my Savior, for putting the desire for Your glory within me, as part of my new birth in Christ. "All you have made will praise you, O LORD; your saints will extol you. They will tell of the glory of your kingdom and speak of your might, so that all men may know of your mighty acts and the glorious splendor of your kingdom. Your kingdom is an everlasting kingdom, and your dominion endures through all generations. " Psalm 145:10-13

O God Most High, God of majesty, how great will be Your glory in the days and ages to come! "All the nations you have made will come and worship before you, O LORD; they will bring glory to your name." Psalm 86:9

"May the peoples praise you, O God; may all the peoples praise you." Psalm 67:3

OVERWHELMED

Apparently God delights to display for us His wisdom in creation. Doing so was a turning point in the saga of Job, that great man of God. After Job reached the point of saying, "It profits a man nothing when he tries to please God" (Job 34:9), the Lord confronted him directly with a series of questions designed to put Job in his place—to remind him of the vast gulf between himself and God. "Who is this that darkens my counsel with words without knowledge?" the Lord asked. "Brace yourself like a man; I will question you, and you shall answer me" (38:2-3).

What follows (in chapters 38–41) is a most remarkable passage that I commend to you as another "gallery" of God's creative wisdom and power. To overwhelm Job with a sense of His greatness, God used His creation as a vivid demonstration.

What was Job's response? He first says, "I am unworthy—how can I reply to you? I put my hand over my mouth. I spoke once, but I have no answer—twice, but I

will say no more" (40:4-5). Job in effect surrenders. He rec-
ognizes God's absolute majesty.

But God isn't through. He continues to bombard Job
with questions designed to both humble Job and exalt Himself. Finally Job responds:

> *I know that you can do all things;*
>> *no plan of yours can be thwarted....*
> *Surely I spoke of things I did not understand,*
>> *things too wonderful for me to know....*
> *My ears had heard of you*
>> *but now my eyes have seen you.*
> *Therefore I despise myself*
>> *and repent in dust and ashes. (42:2-3,5-6)*

Job acknowledges God's sovereignty—"no plan of yours
can be thwarted"; and His wisdom—"I spoke of things I
did not understand, things too wonderful for me to know."
But most of all he experiences a sudden and significant
growth in his fear of God. Job already had been commended
by the Lord Himself as "a man who fears God" (Job 1:8);
now, through seeing the Lord's wisdom and power in creation, he comes to fear Him even more.

I hope you and I will not have to go through trials as
intense as Job's. But we can learn from him to fear the Lord

as we, too, see God's wisdom and power displayed in His theater of creation.

Thank You, Lord, for reminding me that "the fear of the LORD is the beginning of wisdom." Psalm 111:10

Like Job, I, too, am unworthy to come before You. Like Job, I, too, must surrender to You. Like Job, I, too, recognize Your absolute majesty.

In my heart and mind, let me be still and know that You are God. In this quiet moment, I worship You. In quiet reverence I acknowledge Your sovereignty and Your wisdom. Yes, it is true: "You can do all things; no plan of yours can be thwarted." Your thoughts and plans and deeds truly are "things too wonderful for me to know." Psalm 46:10; Job 42:2-3

"My heart is not proud, O LORD, my eyes are not haughty; I do not concern myself with great matters or things too wonderful for me. But I have stilled and quieted my soul; like a weaned child with its mother, like a weaned child is my soul within me." Psalm 131:1-2

In this quietness and trust, I long for You, O God. "As the deer pants for streams of water, so my soul pants for you, O God. My soul thirsts for God, for the living God." Isaiah 30:15; Psalm 42:1-2

O living God, "I spread out my hands to you; my soul thirsts for you like a parched land." Psalm 143:6

How I thank You for the blood of Christ that cleans my conscience from acts that lead to death, so that I may serve You, O living God! Thank You for the blood of Christ that gives me confidence to enter Your Most Holy Place, now and forever. Hebrews 9:14; 10:19-20

THE WONDERS
OF HIS PROVIDENCE

God's providence is His constant care for and His absolute rule over all His creation, directing all things to their appointed end for His own glory. Note that His providence embraces two activities: caring for His creation and governing it. Both have His glory as their goal, and in both we see His wisdom.

God *cares* for His creation. Psalm 104—which describes many facets of creation and states, "In wisdom you made them all" (verse 24)—goes on to praise God's care over all of nature. We read that "He makes grass grow for the cattle, and plants for man to cultivate" (verse 14), and that His creatures "all look to you to give them food at the proper time" (verse 27).

His Fatherly care is mentioned throughout Scripture. Here are a few examples: "He himself gives all men life and breath" (Acts 17:25). "He…supplies seed to the sower and bread for food" (2 Corinthians 9:10). He "[endows] the heart with wisdom [and gives] understanding to the mind" (Job 38:36). He teaches the farmer practical wisdom (Isaiah 28:23-28).

From these last two passages and others we can reasonably infer that all practical wisdom in every field of endeavor comes from God. It may come by way of parents, teachers, or mentors, but it all originated ultimately with God. He is not only infinite in His own wisdom, but He is the source of all the finite wisdom we possess. Endowing mankind with all manner of skills and practical wisdom for living on this earth is all part of God's care for the world.

God also *governs* His universe, not only inanimate creation, but also the actions of both men and animals. He is called "the ruler of all things" (1 Chronicles 29:12). "He does as he pleases with the powers of heaven and the peoples of the earth. No one can hold back his hand or say to him: 'What have you done?'" (Daniel 4:35). Our plans depend entirely on Him: "Who can speak and have it happen if the Lord has not decreed it?" (Lamentations 3:37). James instructs us to say, "If it is the Lord's will, we will live and do this or that" (James 4:15).

God's rule is universal and absolute. No one can act outside of God's will or against it. Nothing is too large or small to escape His governing hand. A sparrow cannot fall to the ground without His will (Matthew 10:29); not one drop of rain falls without His command (Amos 4:7). The mighty Babylonian Empire falls in one night because of God's sovereign judgment against it (Daniel 4:22-30). In all of God's rule over creation, Calvin says, "He directs everything by his incomprehensible wisdom and disposes it to his own end."[30]

But God's wisdom is not as apparent to us in providence as it is in creation. He works in providence by an unseen hand. He works through what we call secondary causes—the actions of people and other living creatures, as well as the so-called laws of nature. God often governs His universe through unwitting and even unwilling instruments.

The cry of a baby saved the Jewish nation from destruction and ultimately changed the course of history. The decree of a Roman emperor that a census should be taken caused another baby to be born in Bethlehem, rather than in Nazareth, thus fulfilling God's prophecy. Neither baby Moses nor Caesar Augustus had any intention of carrying out God's providence, but both acted under His sovereign prompting.

God raised up the Assyrian army to punish His people, and calls it "the rod of my anger, in whose hand is the club of my wrath!" Yet Scripture expressly says of the Assyrian ruler, "But this is not what he intends, this is not what he has in mind" (Isaiah 10:5,7). The Assyrian king had no thought of carrying out God's will; his intention was to conquer nations. But God used him to do His bidding.

God even caused two cows to act contrary to natural instincts and return the ark of the covenant from Philistine territory to Israel (1 Samuel 6:1-12). Whether it's a baby, the ruler of an empire, a cow, or the seemingly blind forces of nature, God has a limitless supply of agents and instruments at His disposal and through which He governs His creation by His unseen hand.

A classic example of God's using unwitting instruments to fulfill His purpose is the action of Joseph's brothers in selling him into slavery (Genesis 37:12-36). They intended only to give vent to their jealous hatred against him. Yet Joseph could later assure them, "It was not you who sent me here, but God" (45:8).

Years later, after their father died, Joseph said to his brothers, "You intended to harm me, but God intended it for good to accomplish what is now being done, the saving of many lives" (50:20). The sinful brothers intended one thing; God intended another. Both accomplished their purposes, but God used the brothers' sinful actions to save many lives. God's invisible hand is guided by unerring wisdom and ingenious plans.

"O Lord, open my lips, and my mouth will declare your praise." Psalm 51:15

Thank You, Lord God, for Your wise care and control of all creation.

I praise You because Your care of all things is constant and perfect. I give thanks to You, for You are good, and Your faithful love and merciful kindness endure forever. Psalm 136

I praise You because Your control of all things is also constant and perfect. Yes, I give thanks to You, for You are good, and Your faithful love and merciful kindness endure forever.

You have indeed made "everything beautiful in its time." Ecclesiastes 3:11

Thank You especially for the riches of Your grace in Jesus Christ which You have "lavished on us with all wisdom and understanding." Ephesians 1:7-8

Gracious Father, I give thanks to You, for You are good; Your faithful love and Your merciful kindness endure forever.

"Praise the LORD. Praise the LORD, O my soul. I will praise the LORD all my life; I will sing praise to my God as long as I live." Psalm 146:1-2

A MYSTERY TOO HIGH

One reason we may not recognize God's wisdom in providence is because He often works in ways contrary to how we would. His wisdom and ways are so much higher than ours that we can't understand them. He tells us that our thoughts and ways simply are not His, and adds, "As the heavens are higher than the earth, so are my ways higher than your ways and my thoughts than your thoughts" (Isaiah 55:8-9). The implication in this passage, writes Edward J. Young,

> is that just as the heavens are so high above the earth that by human standards their height cannot be measured, so also are God's ways and thoughts so above those of man that they cannot be grasped by man in their fullness. In other words, the ways and thoughts of God are incomprehensible to man. Even though God reveals them to man, he cannot fully understand them; to him they are incomprehensible.[31]

Imagine a certain family with two sons: Joe, fifteen, and Sammy, only four. Joe plays ball with Sammy, wrestles with him, and takes him on walks. But one summer Joe goes away on a ten-week missions trip. The boys' father has actively promoted the trip, encouraged Joe to go, and helped him raise the necessary funds.

As the summer goes by, Sammy is missing his brother a lot. Finally one day he says to his dad, "Why did you send Joe away?"

To answer, Dad could talk about Joe's gaining a vision for world missions, learning to serve others, trusting God to supply the necessary funds, and being a good team member. But Sammy wouldn't understand. Those concepts, readily apparent to you and me, would pass right over his head. He would have neither the capacity nor the experience to grasp what his dad was explaining.

This is what Edward J. Young is saying about our inability to understand God's ways. My illustration, though, doesn't do full justice. The difference between a four-year-old's understanding and ours, though great, is not infinite. In the normal course of growth, he will someday be able to understand with the same insight we have.

God's wisdom, however, is infinite; ours is finite. This absolute difference is one that I think we fail to grasp. We tend to assume we *would* understand if God would just explain. We don't really believe that "his understanding *no one can fathom*" (Isaiah 40:28).

When Jesus walked with the two disciples on the road to Emmaus, they said to Him, "But we had hoped that he was the one who was going to redeem Israel" (Luke 24:21). That is exactly what had happened, but the two disciples could not see it. God did not work the way they would have worked, so they failed to understand what He was doing. God had even foretold through Moses and the prophets what He was going to do, but the disciples—all of them, not just these two—simply could not comprehend the wisdom of God.

We like the story of Joseph because it ends well and allows us to see God's hidden purpose as He directed the malicious acts of the brothers to accomplish His end. But other situations bother us a bit.

Jesus gave us the Great Commission to make disciples of all nations (Matthew 28:19-20). Several years ago leaders of four missionary radio ministries met together to map out a strategy for broadcasting the gospel by radio to all the remaining unreached peoples of the world. Each organization accepted the responsibility to reach out to certain groups. Within a year, however, one of the broadcasters was off the air due to civil war in its country of operation.

What was God doing? Hadn't He given us the Great Commission? Weren't these organizations seeking to obey His command to make disciples of all nations? Why would

He allow a civil war to frustrate a major part of their strategy for obedience? We don't know what God was doing. We do know that God governs His universe, but in ways infinitely higher than our ways.

It has helped me to consider an unexplained setback in Paul's missionary strategy. Paul had gone to Jerusalem, after which he planned to sail for Rome and then to Spain. In Jerusalem he was illegally arrested at the instigation of the Jews and finally ended up in prison in Caesarea. There he stayed for *two whole years* because Felix, the Roman governor, wanted to grant a favor to the Jews (Acts 24:27). Here was God's leading cross-cultural missionary and church planter languishing in prison when he could have been on his way to Rome and Spain. He finally got to Rome, but as a prisoner. We don't know if he ever made it to Spain.

Why would God do this? Why would He allow His chosen apostle to the Gentiles to sit in prison for two years? God hasn't told us. His ways are higher than ours.

Humility should be a hallmark of those who fear and worship God. To accept that God's ways are often mysterious, that His wisdom is infinite and ours only finite, is an important expression of humility. Then we can say with David, "My heart is not proud, O LORD, my eyes are not haughty; I do not concern myself with great matters or things too wonderful for me" (Psalm 131:1).

Father in heaven, I praise and thank You for how Your wisdom and Your ways are so infinitely high and exalted and incomprehensible. You are truly God Most High!

"You, O LORD, are the Most High over all the earth." "You alone are the Most High." "I will be glad and rejoice in you; I will sing praise to your name, O Most High." Psalms 97:9; 83:18; 9:2

"How awesome is the LORD Most High, the great King over all the earth!" Your "understanding has no limit," and Your "greatness no one can fathom." Psalms 47:2; 147:5; 145:3

It is true that we "cannot understand the work of God, the Maker of all things." You indeed perform "great things beyond our understanding." And though I can never truly comprehend Your ways, yet I know and believe that they are perfectly right. I praise and exalt and glorify You as the King of heaven, because everything You do is right, all Your ways are impartially just, and those who walk in pride You are more than able to humble. Ecclesiastes 11:5; Job 37:5; Daniel 4:37

"Just and true are your ways, King of the ages." "Yes, Lord God Almighty, true and just are your judgments." Revelation 15:3; 16:7

"As for God, his way is perfect." Yes, You are perfectly good and wise in all You do! "O LORD, you are my God; I will exalt you and praise your name, for in perfect faithfulness you have done marvelous things, things planned long ago." Psalm 18:30; Isaiah 25:1

WISDOM'S CLIMAX

If creation is the theater in which God displays His glorious wisdom, and if the various outworkings of providence represent the drama played out, then the redemptive mission of Christ is the climactic act. God's intention, Paul wrote, "was that now, through the church, the *manifold wisdom* of God should be made known to the rulers and authorities in the heavenly realms, according to his eternal purpose which he accomplished in Christ Jesus our Lord" (Ephesians 3:10-11).

The church, as the object of Christ's redemptive work, is intended to display God's manifold wisdom. This word *manifold* has the idea of multicolored or iridescent, producing a rainbowlike effect. It calls attention to the infinite diversity and sparkling beauty of God's wisdom as displayed in the entire drama of Christ's life, death, and resurrection and the consequent ingathering of people from all nations and all stations of life into one body of Christ.

It is only in Christ and His work that we see God's justice reconciled with mercy, His law reconciled with grace, His holiness with His love, and His power with His compassion. It is only in Christ that unworthy people are both humbled and exalted, and that formerly hostile Jews and Gentiles are reconciled and brought together into one body.

In our Lord's crucifixion, the most momentous event in all history, God displayed in a special way His glorious wisdom in using the acts of sinful men to carry out His plan. The disciples acknowledged this in their prayer recorded in Acts 4:27-28.

> *Indeed Herod and Pontius Pilate met together with the Gentiles and the people of Israel in this city to conspire against your holy servant Jesus, whom you anointed. They did what your power and will had decided beforehand should happen.*

They all did what God decided beforehand should happen. The Roman government and the Jewish leaders conspired together. They thought they were getting rid of a religious troublemaker. Instead they were simply stagehands in the world's greatest drama: the redemption of a people for God from every tribe and language and nation.

But the drama doesn't end at the Cross or even with the Resurrection. Christ's redemptive work must be applied to people's hearts. Throughout the centuries God has been calling them to salvation through an infinite diversity of ways and circumstances, all displaying His wisdom. In my own case I think of a conversation I overheard in which I was not even a participant, but which God used to bring me to Christ.

Now through His Spirit—and in a way we cannot understand—Christ dwells in us and we in Him. All this is from God and the outworking of His wisdom: "It is because of him that you are in Christ Jesus, who has become for us wisdom from God—that is, our righteousness, holiness and redemption" (1 Corinthians 1:30).

"Praise be to my Rock! Exalted be God, the Rock, my Savior!" "You have delivered me from death and my feet from stumbling, that I may walk before God in the light of life." 2 Samuel 22:47; Psalm 56:13

Savior God, I praise You for the infinite depth and beauty of Your wisdom displayed in the life and death and resurrection and glorification of Your precious Son, Jesus Christ. And thank You for giving me Your Holy Spirit, who "searches all things, even the deep things of God," so that through the Holy Spirit's presence within me I might understand the wisdom of all You have freely given me in Christ. 1 Corinthians 2:10-12

I thank You that in Jesus Your Son "are hidden all the treasures of wisdom and knowledge." Your good wisdom in

Your Son is so infinite that every promise You have ever made finds its "yes" in Christ. Thank You for making Christ my wisdom—my righteousness, my holiness, my redemption. Thank You for meeting all my needs according to Your glorious riches in Christ Jesus. Thank You, gracious God! Colossians 2:2-3; 2 Corinthians 1:20; 1 Corinthians 1:30-31; Philippians 4:19

EVERYTHING ORCHESTRATED FOR GOOD

Now look again at God's providence as it applies to His people. Earlier I defined God's providence as "His constant care for and His absolute rule over all His creation, directing all things to their appointed end for His own glory." It's appropriate now to add a final phrase: "and for the good of His people." God's providence is both for His glory *and* for the good of His people. He has designed His eternal purpose so that His glory and our good are inextricably bound together.

This grand truth gives substance to that bedrock promise in Romans 8:28—"God causes all things to work together for good to those who love God, to those who are called according to His purpose" (NASB). This takes us back again to the mystery of God's providence. How can God cause *all* things—the good and the bad, the big things and the little things—to work together for our good?

The *good* mentioned in Romans 8:28 is explained in the next verse as conformity to the likeness of Christ. We have our own idea of what good is, and it seldom includes difficulties and heartaches. But the psalmist said, "It was *good* for me to be afflicted so that I might learn your decrees" (Psalm 119:71). And the writer of Hebrews said, "God disciplines us for our *good,* that we may share in his holiness" (12:10). God causes all of life's circumstances and events, including discipline and affliction, to work together for our good—to conform us to Christ.

Consider the sheer breadth of God's wisdom in bringing this about. Every event of your life—everything you do, everything that happens to you—is somehow woven together into a fabric that is making you more Christlike. There are millions of such events in your life each year, and God orchestrates them all for your good.

But you're just one person. No one knows how many true Christians there are in the world, but let's assume about one billion (out of six billion people). Multiply that number by the millions of events occurring in each believer's life every year and you see the sheer magnitude of God's work. Only an infinite mind—and I truly mean *infinite*—is sufficient for such a task.

Consider the depth of God's wisdom in conforming us to Christ. We're all desperately sinful. In the words of the venerable J. C. Ryle, our best deeds are no more than splendid sins. We might say God has a big job to do in each of us. But He who named a hundred billion times a hundred billion stars and keeps them all in their respective courses can also cause everything in my life and in yours to conform each of us to Christ.

I praise You, infinitely wise God, for the perfect way You cause all things to work together for good to those who love You and who are called according to Your purpose. I praise You for Your infinite skill and wisdom in doing this not only for me, but simultaneously for all Your sons and daughters throughout the world, moment by moment, in every single circumstance of our lives. Romans 8:28

"Ah, Sovereign LORD.... Nothing is too hard for you." How amazingly true it is that "your eyes are open to all the ways of men." And in Your perfect awareness of all things, You perfectly control all circumstances, including all the myriad details of my life. "Many, O LORD my God, are the wonders you have done. The things you planned for us no one can recount to you; were I to speak and tell of them, they would be too many to declare." Jeremiah 32:17,19; Psalm 40:5

Thank You that You are perfectly at work in my life to will and to act according to Your good purpose. In all my circumstances, "you have assigned me my portion and my cup; you have made my lot secure." Philippians 2:13; Psalm 16:5

In my circumstances today, I give you thanks even for obstacles and frustrations. I trust in You, no matter how painfully difficult those circumstances become. 1 Thessalonians 5:18; Job 13:15

Thank You that even when my trials bring grief, I can still be assured that You designed them to prove the genuineness of faith, and to cause my faith in the end to result in "praise, glory and honor when Jesus Christ is revealed." Help me learn to rejoice when I share in Christ's sufferings, that I "may be overjoyed when his glory is revealed." 1 Peter 1:6-7; 4:13

How I praise You that I bear the precious name of Jesus Christ! Help me never to be ashamed of it, especially if I am called to suffer for His sake. 1 Peter 4:16

I rejoice in Your perfect will for my life, now and forever. "You have made known to me the path of life; you will fill me with joy in your presence, with eternal pleasures at your right hand." Psalm 16:11

WANTING MY TRUST—
NOT MY ADVICE

In Isaiah 40 we pictured God's infinite greatness in holding the waters in the hollow of His hand and weighing the mountains on scales. In the same passage Isaiah asks these questions about God's wisdom:

> *Who has understood the mind of the LORD,*
> *or instructed him as his counselor?*
> *Whom did the LORD consult to enlighten him,*
> *and who taught him the right way?*
> *Who was it that taught him knowledge*
> *or showed him the path of understanding?*
> *(40:13-14)*

Who instructed God? Whom did He consult? Think of what we've learned about the design of the human body—the amazing intricacy and efficiency of a single cell, the sheer magnitude of the connecting fibers between nerve cells in the brain. Who could have served as the Lord's consultant on a design task like that? Could you or I?

It's an absurd question, isn't it? Yet we continually want to be God's adviser in His providential workings. We continually want to tell Him how certain circumstances should be changed. Or worse, we question God's wisdom when we can't understand what He's doing.

God's ways are mysterious. But with Paul we can learn to exult in this with praise:

> *How fathomless the depths of God's resources, wisdom, and knowledge! How unsearchable His decisions, and how mysterious His methods! For who has ever understood the thoughts of the Lord, or has ever been His adviser?... Glory to Him forever! (Romans 11:33-36, Charles B. Williams translation)*

To this end may the following words from J. L. Dagg encourage us:

> *It should fill us with joy that infinite wisdom guides the affairs of the world. Many of its events are shrouded in darkness and mystery, and inextricable confusion sometimes seems to reign. Often wickedness prevails, and God seems to have forgotten the creatures that he has made. Our own path through life is dark and devious, and beset with*

difficulties and dangers. How full of consolation is the doctrine that infinite wisdom directs every event, brings... light out of darkness, and, to those who love God, causes all things, whatever be their present aspect and apparent tendency, to work together for good.[32]

So with joy and consolation let us stand in awe of the infinite wisdom of God manifested in creation, providence, and redemption. But let's do more. One of the marks of a God-fearing person is trust in the Lord: "The LORD delights in those who fear him, who put their hope in his unfailing love" (Psalm 147:11). To hope in His unfailing love is to trust Him. As we stand in awe, let us trust Him, even when we don't understand what He is doing.

"I trust in you, O LORD; I say, 'You are my God.' My times are in your hands." [Psalm 31:14-15]

I trust in you, O Lord. "Into your hands I commit my spirit." [Psalm 31:5]

I trust in You, O Lord; I praise You, and I give thanks to You, for You are my light and my salvation and the stronghold of my life. "I love you, O LORD, my strength." [Psalms 27:1; 18:1]

I love You, O Lord. Help me not to depend on the wisdom of the world, for it is foolishness in Your sight. Help me to embrace instead Your wisdom, "the wisdom that comes from heaven," the wisdom that "is first of all pure; then peace-loving, considerate, submissive, full of mercy and good fruit, impartial and sincere." 1 Corinthians 3:19; James 3:17

I love You, O Lord. "Teach me to do your will, for you are my God; may your good Spirit lead me on level ground." Do this, wise Father, for Your name's sake. Psalm 143:10-11

I love You, O Lord, my strength, and I trust in You. "My flesh and my heart may fail, but God is the strength of my heart and my portion forever." Psalm 73:26

"Be exalted, O LORD, in your strength." Psalm 21:13

O God, perfect in wisdom, O Lord my loving Father, I exalt You.

O infinite God! Who has understood Your mind or instructed You as Your counselor? Before the universe was created it existed in all its intricate complexity in Your vast mind. Even the tiny cells in our bodies testify to the sheer brilliance of Your creative genius.

But while we marvel at Your creation, we confess that we often wonder at Your providence. Help us to learn that Your ways truly are higher than our ways, and that You are always working for our good despite the many things we don't understand. May we fear You by trusting You.

And may we ever praise You through Jesus our Lord and Savior.

Amen.

Part IV

For Your Love,
O Lord, I Exalt You

Whoever is wise, let him heed these things
and consider the great love of the LORD.

PSALM 107:43

I will tell of the kindnesses of the LORD,
the deeds for which he is to be praised,
according to all the LORD has done for us—
yes, the many good things he has done…
according to his compassion and many kindnesses.

ISAIAH 63:7

A HEALTHY TENSION

What is God's greatest attribute? I once listened to a series of conference messages on the attributes of God. The first speaker said, "I know it's wrong to exalt one attribute above another, but if we could, I would exalt the holiness of God." The next speaker said, "I know it's wrong to exalt one of God's attributes above another, but if we could, I would exalt the sovereignty of God." As I listened I thought to myself, *And I would exalt the love of God.*

Of course all three of us would be wrong. As the two speakers said, we should not exalt any of God's attributes above the others. All of them, in their infiniteness, are essential to His being. Take away any one of them—say, His omnipotence—and God ceases to be God. God minus omnipotence is not God, just as God minus holiness is not God.

Having said that, there's something about the love of God that should astound us as sinners. His greatness causes us to stand in awe. His holiness lays us prostrate in the dust. His wisdom calls forth our admiration. But His love, rightly understood, causes us to gasp in amazement. It's not without reason that Charles Wesley penned those memorable words, "Amazing love! How can it be that Thou my God shouldst die for me?" We can understand God's love to a worthy object, but it's the fact that He loves sinners that so astonishes us.

In the physical realm there are two opposing forces called *centrifugal* and *centripetal.* Centrifugal force tends to pull away from a center of rotation, while centripetal force pulls toward the center. A stone whirled about on the end of a string exerts centrifugal force on the string, while the string exerts centripetal force on the stone. Each of these forces cannot exist without the other. Take away one and the other immediately disappears.

These two opposing forces can help us understand something of our relationship with God. The centrifugal force represents those attributes of God such as His holiness and sovereignty that cause us to bow in awe and self-abasement before Him. They hold us reverently distant from the One who, by the simple power of His word, created the universe out of nothing.

The centripetal force represents the love of God. It surrounds us with grace and mercy and draws us with cords of love into the Father's warm embrace. To properly fear and worship God we must understand and respond to both these forces.

The fear of God certainly denotes the only fitting response to His awesome greatness and transcendent majesty. It's also a recognition of our own frailty, weakness, and sinfulness in the presence of His sovereign power and infinite holiness. At the same time, the fear of God also denotes the love and humble gratitude of the person who, conscious of his own sinfulness and exposure to divine wrath, has experienced the grace and mercy of God in the forgiveness of his sins.

This aspect of the fear of God is beautifully expressed in Psalm 130:3-4.

> *If you, O LORD, kept a record of sins,*
> *   O Lord, who could stand?*
> *But with you there is forgiveness;*
> *   therefore you are feared.*

Here it is not the dread of divine wrath, but rather gratitude for divine forgiveness that draws forth from the psalmist the response he calls fear.

Both these attitudes—awe and gratitude—are necessary to a proper expression of the fear of God. Just as the centrifugal and centripetal forces cannot exist independently, so neither awe nor gratitude alone can represent adequately the biblical meaning of the fear of the Lord.

Sometimes we will sense one more strongly than the other. We may on occasion experience overwhelming awe as God reveals Himself to our hearts in His majesty, or we may experience inexpressible gratitude as we encounter His mercy. Cherish those moments, but seek to maintain a balance between awe and gratitude.

There should always be a healthy tension between the confidence with which we come before God as His children and the reverential awe with which we behold Him as our sovereign Lord. There's a difference between holy familiarity and unholy familiarity with God. We have indeed received the Spirit of adoption, the Spirit by whom we cry, "*Abba,* Father" (Romans 8:15). This expression conveys the warmth and confidence with which we may come into His presence.

At the same time we should remember that this One whom we're invited to address as our Father is still the sovereign and holy God. He is still the King who is eternal, immortal, and invisible, and who lives in unapproachable light, whom no one has seen or can see (1 Timothy 1:17, 6:16).

To seek this healthy tension myself, I like to begin my private worship each morning with words such as these:

> *Sovereign God of all creation, I come to You today through*
> *Jesus Christ, and through Him I call You Father. I ac-*

knowledge that in myself I'm the worst of sinners, but through Christ Jesus I'm Your son.

With that opening prayer I seek to capture both the awe and the intimacy with which we should all relate to God.

Yes, Lord, through Jesus Christ alone I come to You in worship today. Through Jesus alone I desire to continually offer You a sacrifice of praise—the fruit of lips that confess Your name. Hebrews 13:15

I enter Your gates with thanksgiving and Your courts with praise. I give thanks to You and praise Your name, for You are good and Your love endures forever, Your faithfulness through all generations. Psalm 100:4-5

I worship You as the holy, sovereign God; You are infinitely above and apart from me and all Your creation. I also worship You as my loving Father who draws me ever closer in Your embrace. All this is true of You, awesome Father—"You, O God, are strong…you, O LORD, are loving." Psalm 62:11-12

In the coming days, as You continue working in my spirit, I ask You especially to "show the wonder of your great love, you who save by your right hand those who take refuge in you." Show me more and more how awesome and amazing Your love really is. "For great is your love, higher than the heavens; your faithfulness reaches to the skies." Psalms 17:7; 108:4

Loving Father, I worship You as the source of every single blessing in my life. "You are my Lord; apart from you I have no good thing." "All my fountains are in you." I have nothing that I did not receive from You. Psalms 16:2; 87:7; 1 Corinthians 4:7

"Let the name of the LORD be praised, both now and forevermore." Psalm 113:2

THE FATHER'S PAIN

We've looked at God's greatness, holiness, and wisdom, attributes that convey the great distance between us and God. Each of them should stimulate a tremendous sense of awe in our hearts. Now to balance this we need to give attention to the force of God's love drawing us near, that our hearts might be lifted up in wondrous adoration.

The apostle John said, "God is love" (1 John 4:8)—just three simple words, yet this is one of the Bible's most profound statements. It says more than that God is loving. We might say that of another person. But only of God can we say, He is love. This statement speaks of God's essential nature.

John makes it clear, however, that love is not simply an abstract quality of God. Rather His love is active, for John goes on to say, "This is how God showed his love among us: He sent his one and only Son into the world that we might live through him. This is love: not that we loved God, but that he loved us and sent his Son as an atoning sacrifice for our sins" (1 John 4:9-10).

God *showed* His love by *sending* His Son. This reminds us immediately of the familiar words of John 3:16, "For God so loved the world that He gave his one and only Son." This statement is repeated so often, I fear we tend to take it for granted. It doesn't stir us much anymore. How can we recapture that sense of amazement that Charles Wesley wrote about?

One story in the Bible helps us especially to appreciate more of what God did when He gave His one and only Son to die in our place. In Genesis 22:2, God said to Abraham, "Take your son, your only son, Isaac, whom you love, and go to the region of Moriah. Sacrifice him there as a burnt offering on one of the mountains I will tell you about." Remember that Isaac was a "miracle baby," born when Abraham was a hundred years old and his wife, Sarah, was ninety. Moreover Isaac was the child of promise through whom God had said Abraham would become the father of many nations (17:5).

Try to put yourself in Abraham's place and feel something of his astonishment and pain. Surely he must have felt as if a dagger had been driven into his heart. But God doesn't just drive the dagger in—He twists it by His use of three descriptive terms.

God refers to Isaac as Abraham's *only* son. (In recounting this incident, the writer of Hebrews uses the expression "one and only son" [11:17] to make it more emphatic.)

Abraham had waited years for this son, and now God tells him to slay him and burn him upon an altar of sacrifice on some distant mountain.

God also calls the son by name, *Isaac*—the name He Himself had given the boy before he was born.

Then He adds the piercing phrase *whom you love.* God seems to go out of His way to remind Abraham how special this son is. Abraham needed no reminders, but we get the idea God wants him to experience the pain as deeply as possible.

Why did God do this? The opening line to this story tells us that God "tested" Abraham (22:1). He tested both his obedience (22:18) and his faith (Hebrews 11:17). But I believe God also did it to help us understand a little of what it cost Him to send His only Son for us.

The parallels between Isaac and Jesus help us see how remarkably Isaac prefigured Jesus. Jesus is also called God's "one and only Son." He, too, was named by God before He was born (Matthew 1:21). And twice God's voice comes from heaven saying, "This is my Son, *whom I love;* with him I am well pleased" (Matthew 3:17, 17:5). Abraham's love for Isaac, great as it was, was still imperfect. God's love for His Son is perfect and hence a greater love. Abraham's love for Isaac was only a shadow of the Father's love for Jesus.

Along with the parallels, however, there is one significant difference. As they neared the mountain, Isaac said to his father, "Where is the lamb for the burnt offering?" Abraham answered, "God himself will provide the lamb for the burnt offering." As the scene is played out, God provided a ram to be offered instead of Isaac. But there could be no substitute for Jesus. Only He could die on that cruel cross to pay for our sins. Abraham did not have to go through with such a heart-wrenching deed—but God did.

God Himself laid our sins on Christ (Isaiah 53:6). God Himself made Him who had no sin to be sin for us (2 Corinthians 5:21). But this doesn't mean God did not in some way feel a father's pain. We have to be careful in attributing emotional pain to God. It's certainly true that God, being sovereign, can never experience the same pain we do when we are victimized by the hurtful actions of someone else. God's blessedness is eternally undisturbed. Yet it's difficult to think He observed His own dear Son crucified by wicked men without feeling a father's pain, only far more deeply than what Abraham felt.

There's still another important difference in the stories of Isaac and Jesus. Abraham was prepared to sacrifice his son in obedience to the command of the loving God whom he worshiped. God sacrificed His Son to save an unloving people who by nature are hostile to Him and rebellious against Him. Scripture says that God "did not spare his own Son, but gave him up for us all" (Romans 8:32). God spared

Abraham's son, but did not spare His own. What amazing, unfathomable love, that the eternal, sovereign, holy God should sacrifice His Son for sinners such as you and me! May we never again think of the story of Abraham and Isaac without finding within it a picture of God's great love for us.

Father, You are love, and for this I praise You.

You paid a painful price to prove Your love, and for this I praise You.

You showed me Your great love by sending Your one and only Son into the world as an atoning sacrifice for my sins, that through Him I might live. This is love! This is perfect love, awesome love, astounding love. This is You! 1 John 4:8-10

Thank You, mighty God, for loving me into Your salvation. "I will be glad and rejoice in your love, for you saw my affliction and knew the anguish of my soul. You have not handed me over to the enemy but have set my feet in a spacious place." "I will praise you forever for what you have done; in your name I will hope, for your name is good." Psalms 31:7-8; 52:9

I worship and praise You as "the Father of compassion and the God of all comfort." You are "close to the brokenhearted," and You offer salvation to "those who are crushed in spirit." "Your compassion is great, O LORD." 2 Corinthians 1:3; Psalms 34:18; 119:156

Now, O Lord, "continue your love to those who know you." In my life today, deal with me according to Your great compassion. "Remember, O LORD, your great mercy and love, for they are from of old. Remember not the sins of my youth and my rebellious ways; according to your love remember me, for you are good, O LORD." Psalms 36:10; 25:6-7

Yes, Lord, I have tasted and seen that You are good. I worship You. I take refuge in You, and I stay close to You. Psalm 34:8

I worship You as the God of grace, as we fully see and experience in Jesus. You are always giving of Yourself to others, and everything You give Your children is good, and everything good comes only from You. "Every good and perfect gift is from above, coming down from the Father of…lights." In answer to Your children's prayers, You give "generously to all without finding fault." You give grace, "more grace," "surpassing grace." And You promise to give even more grace in the future, "when Jesus Christ is revealed." John 1:16; James 1:17; Matthew 7:11; James 1:5; 4:6; 2 Corinthians 9:14; 1 Peter 1:13

How can I ever thank You enough? You have given me so much!

You are the God "who created the heavens and stretched them out, who spread out the earth and all that comes out of it, who gives breath to its people, and life to those who walk on it." You are the God "who gives life to everything." Isaiah 42:5; 1 Timothy 6:13

Thank You for giving me my voice, my hearing, my sight. Exodus 4:11

Thank You for meeting all my physical needs. You supply "seed to the sower and bread for food." You give "the ability to produce wealth." For "as long as the earth endures," You give "seedtime and harvest, cold and heat, summer and winter, day and night." You give "autumn and spring rains in season." To all mankind You have given us creation as our dominion, with these amazing words—"I now give you everything." Everything! 2 Corinthians 9:10; Deuteronomy 8:18; Genesis 8:22; Jeremiah 5:24; Genesis 9:2-3

Thank You also for meeting the needs of my heart and my spirit. Thank You for giving us Your beautiful rainbow as a sign of Your love. Thank You for giving me "songs in the night." Genesis 9:12-16; Job 35:10

Thank You for all the promised ways You help me in my daily life—for offering me power and strength, wisdom and understanding, endurance and encouragement. Psalm 68:35; Proverbs 2:6; Romans 15:5

Most of all I thank You for Your "indescribable gift"— Your one and only Son. Since You did not spare Your own Son, but gave Jesus up for us all, I know that You will certainly, "along with him, graciously give us all things." All things! 2 Corinthians 9:15; John 3:16; Romans 8:32

Thank You for giving me "the victory through our Lord

Jesus Christ," and for giving me in Christ "the knowledge of the secrets of the kingdom of heaven." 1 Corinthians 15:57; Matthew 13:11

I give thanks especially for my eternal life in Christ. Thank You for giving me faith, repentance, and forgiveness. You are truly "the God who gives life to the dead." Romans 6:23;
1 John 5:11; Ephesians 2:8; Acts 5:31; Romans 4:17

Thank You for generously pouring out Your Holy Spirit upon my life. You are the God who "gives the Spirit without limit." And You give me not only Your Spirit, but also Your Spirit's perfect prayers for me, in accordance with Your will. Titus 3:6; John 3:34; Romans 8:27

"O LORD my God, I will give you thanks forever." Psalm 30:12

GOD'S WRATH AGAINST ME TURNED ASIDE

We still have not begun to comprehend God's love, however, until we understand John's statement that "God…sent his Son as an atoning sacrifice for our sins" (1 John 4:10). A footnote in the NIV translation explains "atoning sacrifice" as that which turns aside God's wrath, taking away our sins. God gave His only Son to die in our place in order to satisfy His justice and thus turn aside His wrath from us.

It's difficult for us to think about the wrath of God. We prefer to concentrate on His love because this is far more congenial to our thinking. Another reason is that we tend to view wrath in human terms. We think of it as strong and sometimes violent anger or fury. We envision a wrathful person as being out of control with his or her emotions.

Though we should never think of God's wrath as uncontrolled, violent passion, the Bible does use strong language to describe it—words such as *anger, fury,* and *indignation.* Jeremiah 32:37 speaks of His "furious anger and great wrath." In Revelation 19:15 we see Jesus treading "the wine-press of the fury of the wrath of God Almighty." To avoid a comparison to human wrath, God's wrath has been defined as His settled determination to punish sin. It is more than that; it's a determination to punish sin with a vengeance. Unrepentant people are said to be "storing up wrath against [themselves] for the day of God's wrath, when his righteous judgment will be revealed" (Romans 2:5). God stores up goodness for those who fear Him (Psalm 31:19), but the unrepentant store up God's wrath for themselves.

We were all born "by nature objects of wrath" (Ephesians 2:3) because we all came into this world under the condemnation of Adam's sin (Romans 5:18-19). The pretty newborn baby girl weighing seven pounds six ounces and measuring eighteen inches long comes into the world an object of God's wrath—not because of her own sin, but because of her identity with Adam in his. All of us then aggravate our condition by daily adding to it our own personal sin, which by its nature would provoke God's wrath if we were not in Christ.

We don't truly appreciate the seriousness of this until we realize that sin—all sin—provokes the wrath of God. But consider God's love in sending His Son as an atoning sacrifice for our sins: On the cross Jesus suffered God's wrath in our place, thereby turning it aside from us. When He cried out, "My God, my God, why have you forsaken me?"

(Matthew 27:46), He was bearing the wrath that was justly due to us. This is the meaning of the atonement. Only as we come to grips with the fact that we truly were objects of God's wrath do we begin to appreciate this good news of the gospel.

It is not enough, however, to appreciate God's love only in terms of our initial salvation. We should be growing each year in our awareness of the depth of His love for us in Christ—as we become more aware of the reality of our own sin even as believers. An increasing understanding of God's holiness, of one's own sin, and the value of Christ's death will always mark a person who's growing as a Christian.

Lutheran pastor Don Matzat wrote, "If you read about the experiences of Christians who progressed in their relationship with the Lord Jesus beyond the norm, you will note the combination of a deep sense of sin and failure together with a deep appreciation for what God accomplished in Christ Jesus."[33] Then he quotes Paul Tournier's observation of two things that increase by degrees and side by side: the awareness of our guilt, and the awareness of God's love.[34]

Some years ago I prayed that God would show me more of His love. He answered that prayer by showing me more of my sin—not just specific sins I'd committed, but the sinfulness of my heart. Then I began to appreciate more His love to me.

This is when we really start to enjoy fearing and worshiping God: when we realize in the depth of our being that we justly deserve the wrath of God, then see that wrath poured out on Jesus instead of on ourselves. We're both awed at His wrath and astonished at His love.

You, O Lord, are "a righteous judge, a God who expresses his wrath every day." Your wrath "is being revealed from heaven against all the godlessness and wickedness of men." Psalm 7:11; Romans 1:18-19

Almighty and Holy God, I acknowledge that You are right to express Your wrath, for all Your works and Your words "are faithful and just.... They are steadfast for ever and ever, done in faithfulness and uprightness." Psalm 111:7-8

I worship You and thank You for providing the atoning sacrifice for Your wrath against me. Thank You for meeting the demands of Your justice in Your Son—"Jesus, who rescues us from the coming wrath." Since I have now been justified by Jesus' blood, how much more shall I be saved through Him from Your wrath! 1 Thessalonians 1:10; Romans 5:9

"How priceless is your unfailing love!" "I will praise you, O Lord my God, with all my heart; I will glorify your name forever. For great is your love toward me; you have delivered me from the depths of the grave." Psalms 36:7; 86:12-13

Yes, *"I will exalt you, O LORD, for you lifted me out of the depths.... O LORD my God, I called to you for help and you healed me."* Psalm 30:1-2

"I will bow down...and will praise your name for your love and your faithfulness." "Because your love is better than life, my lips will glorify you. I will praise you as long as I live, and in your name I will lift up my hands. My soul will be satisfied as with the richest of foods; with singing lips my mouth will praise you." Psalms 138:2; 63:3-5

JESUS DIED FOR *ME*

When John said, "This is how God showed his love among us: He sent his one and only Son" (1 John 4:9), he was obviously referring to God the Father. It was the Father who sent the Son. We must not overlook the love of God the Son, however. John also said, "This is how we know what love is: Jesus Christ laid down his life for us" (1 John 3:16). Though the Father sent the Son, the Son came voluntarily. Though He is indeed God, the second person of the Trinity, He took upon Himself our nature and suffered in our place on the cross because of His love for us.

The apostle Paul personalized Christ's love: "The life I live in the body, I live by faith in the Son of God, who loved me and gave himself for *me*" (Galatians 2:20). It isn't enough to know Christ died for sinners; I must believe He died for me. Then as I see more of my sinfulness, I appreciate more the love of Christ as He bore those sins in my place. The hymn writer Charles Gabriel expressed the awe that leads to this appreciation:

I stand amazed in the presence
Of Jesus the Nazarene,
And wonder how He could love me,
A sinner, condemned, unclean.

When we stand amazed at the Savior's love, we find our-selves motivated to live for Him. "For Christ's love compels us," Paul said in 2 Corinthians 5:14. Compels us to do what? To live no longer for ourselves, but for Him who died for us and was raised again (verse 15). Our obedience is closely linked to—in fact is a tangible expression of—our fear and worship of God. But for this obedience to be pleas-ing to God, it must be motivated by love and gratitude, not by fear of punishment or hope for reward. That's why it's so crucial that our fear of God include a strong element of amazement at His love.

However, we'll be amazed at His love only to the extent we stand in awe of His person. The realization of who He is—Creator and Sustainer of the universe—is what makes Christ's love so amazing.

Suppose you had an urgent need for a person-to-person blood transfusion and your best friend happens to have your blood type. He or she would gladly donate, and it would be a routine matter. Suppose, however, that your blood type was extremely rare, and the president of the United States was one of the few people who happened to have it as well. If the president flew on Air Force One to your city and donated blood to you, it would be a nationally newsworthy event.

One person gives you blood, and no one notices. Another gives you blood, and it makes the evening news. What's the difference?

The difference is in the dignity of the person's position or office. The dignity and prestige of the presidency sets the second person apart, making his donation of blood to you or me an extraordinary event.

Now take that illustration and apply it to our Lord Jesus Christ. Though He comes in humility, He is in fact no ordinary citizen. His status is something that not even the Roman emperor can match. He's the One who created the universe and sustains it by His powerful word (Hebrews 1:1-3). And He has come all the way from heaven's glory to live and die for you and me because of His love.

All that we've studied so far about God in His greatness, holiness, and wisdom applies as much to the Son as to the Father. In fact, on the basis of John 12:38-41 where we learn that Isaiah "saw Jesus' glory," it seems that the Lord whom Isaiah saw in his vision (Isaiah 6:1-8) was the preincarnate Christ. This is what makes Christ's death so amazing—that this Holy One before whom Isaiah is totally devastated should come and die for sinful men and women who are the very antithesis of holiness.

"Praise be to the LORD, for he showed his wonderful love to me." "Surely God is my help; the Lord is the one who sustains me." "I sought the LORD, and he answered me; he delivered me from all my fears." Psalms 31:21; 54:4; 34:4

"Because you are my help, I sing in the shadow of your wings. My soul clings to you; your right hand upholds me." "For you have delivered me from death and my feet from stumbling, that I may walk before God in the light of life." "You are my God, and I will give you thanks; you are my God, and I will exalt you." Psalms 63:7-8; 56:13; 118:28

Jesus, my Lord and my God, I exalt You. I praise You. You are "the Holy One of God," and "the Righteous One," and "the Living One." You are "the Alpha and the Omega…who is, and who was, and who is to come, the Almighty." John 6:69; Acts 22:14; Revelation 1:18; 1:8

You are God! "Truly you are the Son of God!" Your "name is the Word of God." You are "the image of the invisible God." Matthew 14:33; Revelation 19:13; Colossians 1:15

You are the Lord of lords and King of kings, and Your kingdom will never end. "Your throne, O God, will last for ever and ever, and righteousness will be the scepter of your kingdom." You love righteousness and hate wickedness. You are "holy and true." Revelation 17:14; Luke 1:33; Hebrews 1:8-9; Revelation 3:7

And You are "the Lamb of God, who takes away the sin of the world!" John 1:29

O Lamb of God, I worship You. I bow down before You. I glorify You.

"Worthy is the Lamb, who was slain, to receive power and wealth and wisdom and strength and honor and glory and praise!" Revelation 5:12

"To the Lamb be praise and honor and glory and power, for ever and ever!" Revelation 5:13

Amen.

RICH IN GRACE, RICH IN MERCY

In Ephesians 2:1-3 the apostle Paul presents a dismal picture of us before we trusted Christ as Savior:

> *As for you, you were dead in your transgressions and sins, in which you used to live when you followed the ways of this world and of the ruler of the kingdom of the air, the spirit who is now at work in those who are disobedient. All of us also lived among them at one time, gratifying the cravings of our sinful nature and following its desires and thoughts. Like the rest, we were by nature objects of wrath.*

Paul says we were spiritually dead, unable to help ourselves or do anything about our plight. We were not drowning people needing a life buoy—we were dead people in need of life. Further, we were slaves to the world, to the devil, and to our own sinful natures. And as we've already seen, we were by nature objects of God's holy wrath. Dead, slaves, objects of wrath—what a desperate condition!

Against this dark backdrop of sin and misery, Paul gives the solution (verses 4-5):

> But because of his great love for us, God, who is rich in mercy, made us alive with Christ even when we were dead in transgressions—it is by grace you have been saved.

Three key words stand out in this passage: *love, mercy,* and *grace.* Note Paul's superlative language: *great* love, *rich* in mercy, and in verse 7, "the *incomparable* riches of his grace." What a sharp contrast Paul draws between our pitiful condition and God's glorious remedy. God is rich in mercy and rich in grace, and He bountifully bestows both on us because of His great love.

How should we understand the words *grace* and *mercy* as Paul uses them? Think of them as the two arms with which God reaches out in His love to save us. His grace is His arm of love reaching out to us in our guilt, while His mercy is His love reaching out to us in our pitiable condition because of our sin. Both grace and mercy contemplate our sin—grace its guilt, and mercy its misery.

Grace is *God's favor through Christ to people who deserve His wrath.* It is more than the oft-quoted definition of "unmerited favor." God's grace addresses not only our lack of merit, but also our positive *de*merit. It is blessing bestowed in the presence of demerit.

When I was a small child, homeless men (then called hobos) would sometimes appear at our front door and ask my mother for a meal. Without receiving any work in return, mother would prepare a plate of food for them to eat on our front porch. She was granting an unmerited or unearned favor, but it was not grace. If, however, a hobo appeared at our door whom my mother recognized as a man who had previously robbed us, a new element is introduced. Now the food is given despite demerit. Not only is the man undeserving of the food in the sense of earning it; he actually deserves punishment instead because of his crime.

We all stand before God with innumerable counts of demerit against us. It isn't an overstatement to use Ezra's words: "Our sins are higher than our heads and our guilt has reached to the heavens" (Ezra 9:6). We deserve God's wrath. Instead we receive favor, bountiful favor—we're blessed with every spiritual blessing in Christ (Ephesians 1:3). Why?

The answer is in the two words *through Christ* in our definition of grace. Through Christ and His atoning death, we're delivered from the wrath we deserve. And through Christ and His life of obedience for us, we receive the boundless favor we don't deserve.

This favor comes to us in many forms. We're first of all saved by grace (Ephesians 2:8-9), but it doesn't stop there.

Grace is God's power enabling us to cope with life's difficulties (2 Corinthians 12:9). It supplies the strength we need to live the Christian life (2 Timothy 2:1). Grace provides the spiritual gifts by which we serve in the body of Christ (Romans 12:6). Every blessing you receive, every answer to prayer you experience, is an expression of God's grace to you.

All these favors come to us because of the sinless life and sin-bearing death of our Lord. A popular definition of *grace* is the acronym, *G*od's *R*iches *A*t *C*hrist's *E*xpense. Jesus suffered in our place and paid for our sins. He also lived in our place and earned all our blessings.

While grace contemplates our guilt, mercy has regard to our misery, which is the consequence of our sin. God's mercy is more than compassion for someone in need. It is compassion in spite of demerit. If the hobo-robber in the above illustration ended up in a wretched condition in prison, and my mother in various ways sought to relieve his distress, that would begin to picture God's mercy.

But it would be only a faint picture. No misery in this life can begin to compare with the misery of those suffering eternally under the wrath of God. Even the Nazi Holocaust, awful as it was, pales by comparison to the lake of fire of God's judgment.

God is sovereign in extending His mercy. He said to Moses, "I will have mercy on whom I will have mercy, and

I will have compassion on whom I have compassion" (Exodus 33:19, Romans 9:15). *Sovereign* in this sense refers not to God's power but to His right to do as He pleases. Paul is getting at this when he asks, "Does not the potter have the right to make out of the same lump of clay some pottery for noble purposes and some for common use?" (Romans 9:21). We should therefore always be amazed that God extended His mercy to us.

God is likewise sovereign in extending His grace. He was under no obligation to forgive our sins. He could have plunged each of us into hell as He did the angels who sinned (2 Peter 2:4). Instead He sent His Son to turn aside His wrath by satisfying His justice. And He did even more: He also called us by His gospel and through His Spirit to trust in Christ (2 Thessalonians 2:13-14). If you're a believer and your neighbor isn't, this is not due to your superior wisdom or greater insight into the issues of life. It's because of God's grace in calling you to Christ.

The gospel invitation is wide open to all: "*Everyone* who calls on the name of the Lord will be saved" (Romans 10:13). "*Whoever* is thirsty, let him come; and whoever wishes, let him take the free gift of the water of life" (Revelation 22:17). And yet when we come, we discover that we were chosen in Christ before the creation of the world (Ephesians 1:4). That is grace.

*How infinite is Your love, O God! How infinite is Your grace!
How infinite is Your mercy!*

*Holy Father, You have lavished this love on me, so that I
may actually be called Your child. And Your child is exactly
what I am!* 1 John 3:1

*"O my Strength, I sing praise to you; you, O God, are my
fortress, my loving God." "You, O Lord, are a compassionate
and gracious God, slow to anger, abounding in love and
faithfulness."* Psalms 59:17; 86:15

*You are my shepherd, and I shall never be in want. "Even
though I walk through the valley of the shadow of death, I will
fear no evil, for you are with me; your rod and your staff, they
comfort me. You prepare a table before me in the presence of
my enemies. You anoint my head with oil; my cup overflows.
Surely goodness and love will follow me all the days of my
life, and I will dwell in the house of the LORD forever."* Psalm 23

*"To you, O Lord, I lift up my soul. You are forgiving and good,
O Lord, abounding in love to all who call to you." "To your name
be the glory, because of your love and faithfulness."* Psalms 86:4-5; 115:1

*"Praise be to the Lord, to God our Savior, who daily bears
our burdens."* Psalm 68:19

*"I will sing of the LORD's great love forever; with my
mouth I will make your faithfulness known through all
generations."* Psalm 89:1

IN GRACE I STAND

All true believers acknowledge that we're saved by grace (Ephesians 2:8-9). Paul tells us furthermore that we also *stand* in grace (Romans 5:1-2). On a day-to-day basis we stand accepted by God in the same grace by which we were saved.

And the same definition of grace—God's favor through Christ to people who deserve His wrath—applies in our continuing relationship with God as believers. Daily we sin in thought, word, and deed. We never completely love God with all our heart, soul, and mind, and we never fully love our neighbor as ourselves. Each day we deserve God's wrath, but each day we stand before Him in grace, accepted by Him only through the merit of our Lord Jesus Christ.

As B. B. Warfield said, "Though blessed with every spiritual blessing in the heavenlies in Christ, we are still in ourselves just 'miserable sinners': 'miserable sinners' saved by grace to be sure, but 'miserable sinners' still, deserving in ourselves nothing but everlasting wrath."[35] Our best deeds are polluted with sin and are made acceptable to God only through Jesus Christ (1 Peter 2:5). Even as Christians we never earn favor with God by our performance. All His favor still comes to us through Christ.

Amen! & Amen!

Because of this we can be assured of God's unfailing love to us throughout this life and for eternity. We've done nothing to earn His love and can do nothing to forfeit it. His love in Christ is eternal and unconditional. Nothing can separate us from His love, as the apostle Paul put it so eloquently. Do we really believe what Paul says to us here?

> *Who shall separate us from the love of Christ? Shall trouble or hardship or persecution or famine or nakedness or danger or sword? As it is written:*
>
> > *"For your sake we face death all day long;*
> > *we are considered as sheep to be slaughtered."*
>
> *No, in all these things we are more than conquerors through him who loved us. For I am convinced that neither death nor life, neither angels nor demons, neither the present nor the future, nor any powers, neither height nor depth, nor anything else in all creation, will be able to separate us from the love of God that is in Christ Jesus our Lord. (Romans 8:35-39)*

Do we believe that nothing—not even our own sin—can separate us from God's love? This doesn't mean God winks at our sin like the proverbial indulgent grandfather. Rather it means that He has forgiven our sins because of the atoning sacrifice of His Son. God proved His love to us by sending Christ to suffer in our place. Therefore to doubt His love because of our sin is an affront to Him. It says in effect that the merit of Christ's death is not sufficient to cover the demerit of our sin. What an insult to God!

How then should we respond to God's love to us through Christ?

First, we should fear Him. "With you there is forgiveness; therefore you are feared" (Psalm 130:4). Here Sinclair Ferguson's definition of filial fear is helpful: "It is that indefinable mixture of reverence, fear, pleasure, joy and awe which fills our hearts when we realize who God is and what he has done for us."[36] Realizing who God is and what He has done for us will elicit this biblical fear. As we grow in our understanding of God's love for us in Christ, we will more and more "delight in the fear of the LORD" (Isaiah 11:3).

Our second response comes directly from the passage we've been looking at often, 1 John 4. After showing us God's love in sending His Son, John immediately draws the application: "Dear friends, since God so loved us, we also ought to love one another" (verse 11). We've seen that God's love is sacrificial and unconditional. He loved us when we did not love Him. Therefore we have no excuse for not loving one another.

Certainly there are people who are difficult to love. The fact is, we all are to some degree. We don't have the power in ourselves to love the unlovable, but that also is no excuse. We do have the Holy Spirit enabling us to love others as we look to Him.

So we have no excuse not to love one another, and we have the direct command to do so, based on God's love for us. In fact Paul urges us to "live a *life* of love"—our entire life, seven days a week, is to be characterized by love. Like John, Paul bases that exhortation on Christ's love for us (Ephesians 5:1-2). Our love is to be a reflection of His love.

Third, we should seek to obey God and serve Him in every area of life. We "should no longer live for [ourselves] but for him who died for [us] and was raised again" (2 Corinthians 5:15). Or as Paul says elsewhere, we should "in view of God's mercy,…offer [our] bodies as living sacrifices, holy and pleasing to God" (Romans 12:1).

By using the word *should* I'm not seeking to create a sense of obligation or lay a guilt trip on anyone. My desire has been to help you develop such a view of God's love that you can't help but be motivated to fear and worship Him, to love others, and to wholeheartedly obey and serve Him. I want you to experience *joy* in these responses and to grow in that joy more and more as you increase in the knowledge of His love.

My desire is that both you and I will be so overwhelmed by Christ's love that it will indeed compel us to live not for ourselves but for Him. Too often we're compelled not by love but by a sense of duty or obligation. God does not delight in that kind of motive. He delights in our heart response of love. His love to us, and our love to Him in return, work together to produce genuine joy as we fear, worship, and obey God.

By the blood of Your Son Jesus Christ I come before You in worship, O loving Father, my Creator and my God. I know I can come only by Your grace, because You accept me through the merit of Jesus.

Thank You that I can be assured of Your unfailing love throughout my life and for eternity. Thank You that absolutely nothing—not even my own sin—can ever separate me from Your love for me that is in Christ Jesus my Lord. "I trust in your unfailing love; my heart rejoices in your salvation." Romans 8:35-39; Psalm 13:5

Because of Your infinite love, "I will always have hope; I will praise you more and more." Psalm 71:14

Because of Your infinite love, I worship You. "For great is your love, reaching to the heavens; your faithfulness reaches to the skies. Be exalted, O God, above the heavens; let your glory be over all the earth." Psalm 57:10-11

Because of Your infinite love, I pray to You.

"I pray to you, O LORD, in the time of your favor; in your great love, O God, answer me." ^{Psalm 69:13}

Through the indwelling presence of Christ within me, I ask You to make me "rooted and established in love." Give me power "to grasp how wide and long and high and deep is the love of Christ, and to know this love that surpasses knowledge." Let me "live a life of love," just as Christ loved me and gave Himself up for me as a fragrant offering and sacrifice to You. ^{Ephesians 3:17-19; 5:1-2}

Each day, "let the morning bring me word of your unfailing love, for I have put my trust in you. Show me the way I should go, for to you I lift up my soul." This is my prayer for each day, for myself and for those whom I love: "Satisfy us in the morning with your unfailing love, that we may sing for joy and be glad all our days." ^{Psalms 143:8; 90:14}

"Answer me, O LORD, out of the goodness of your love; in your great mercy turn to me." ^{Psalm 69:16}

"May your love and your truth always protect me." "O Sovereign LORD, deal well with me for your name's sake; out of the goodness of your love, deliver me." ^{Psalms 40:11; 109:21}

Father, I rest in Your love, and I praise and worship You, in spirit and in truth.

"Praise be to the LORD forever! Amen and Amen." "Praise be to his glorious name forever; may the whole earth be filled with his glory. Amen and Amen." ^{Psalms 89:52; 72:19}

"To our God and Father be glory for ever and ever. Amen." Philippians 4:20

"To the only God our Savior be glory, majesty, power and authority, through Jesus Christ our Lord, before all ages, now and forevermore! Amen." Jude 25

"Amen! Praise and glory and wisdom and thanks and honor and power and strength be to our God for ever and ever. Amen!" Revelation 7:12

O God our glorious Father! With You there is forgiveness; therefore You are feared. While we were still sinners, objects of Your just and holy wrath, You loved us and sent Your Son to die for us. You reached out in Your mercy to relieve our misery, and in Your grace to forgive our guilt.

And now through Jesus we call You "Abba, Father." Create in our hearts that sense of filial fear that will cause us to worship and adore You because of Your love to us.

Again we praise You through Jesus our Lord.

Amen.

NOTES

1. John Calvin, *Institutes of the Christian Religion,* ed. John T. McNeill; trans. Ford Lewis Battles, 2 vols. (Philadelphia: Westminster, 1960), 1:377.

2. Stephen Charnock, *The Existence and Attributes of God* (1853, reprint, Grand Rapids: Baker, 1979), 1:212.

3. John MacArthur, *The Ultimate Priority* (Chicago: Moody, 1983), 14.

4. A. W. Tozer, *Whatever Happened to Worship?* (Camp Hill, Pa.: Christian Publications, 1985), 26.

5. MacArthur, *The Ultimate Priority,* 104.

6. Charnock, *The Existence and Attributes of God,* 225-6. I am indebted to MacArthur for calling attention to Charnock's statement by quoting it himself.

7. Quoted by Henry A. Boardman, *The "Higher Life" Doctrine of Sanctification Tried by the Word of God* (1877, reprint, Harrisonburg, Va.: Sprinkle Publications, 1996), 268.

8. Arthur Burnet, ed., *The Valley of Vision: A Collection of Puritan Prayers & Devotions* (Carlisle, Pa.: Banner of Truth Trust, n.d.), 148.

9. I acknowledge my indebtedness for some of the insights on Isaiah 40 to commentaries on Isaiah by Joseph A. Alexander (Klock & Klock), Edward J. Young (Eerdmans), and J. Alec Motyer (InterVarsity). While I have not used verbatim quotations from any of them, I have gained insights into the text and have occasionally used words or short, apt expressions from all of them.

10. Edward J. Young, *The Book of Isaiah,* 3 vols. (Grand Rapids: Eerdmans, 1965-72), 1:242-3.

11. Charnock, *The Existence and Attributes of God,* 2:110.

12. J. Alec Motyer, *The Prophecy of Isaiah* (Downers Grove, Ill.: InterVarsity, 1993), 77, note 1.

13. R. C. Sproul, *The Holiness of God* (Wheaton, Ill.: Tyndale, 1985), 55.

14. Arthur W. Pink, *The Attributes of God* (Grand Rapids: Guardian Press, 1975), 11.

15. Charnock, *Existence and Attributes of God,* 111.

16. Louis Berkhof, *Systematic Theology* (Edinburgh: Banner of Truth Trust, 1939), 73.

17. Motyer, *Prophecy of Isaiah,* 77.

18. H. H. Rowley, *The Faith of Israel* (SCM, 1956), 66; as quoted in Motyer, *Prophecy of Isaiah,* 77.

19. Calvin, *Institutes of the Christian Religion,* 1:367.

20. Calvin, *Institutes of the Christian Religion,* 1:367.

21. John Brown, *Expository Discourses on I Peter,* 2 vols. (Edinburgh: Banner of Truth Trust, 1975), 1:472-3.

22. Quoted by Paul Brand and Philip Yancey, *In His Image* (Grand Rapids: Zondervan, 1984), 13.

23. Brand and Yancey, *In His Image,* 58.

24. Paul Brand and Philip Yancey, *Fearfully and Wonderfully Made* (Grand Rapids: Zondervan, 1980), 70.

25. Michael Denton, *Evolution: A Theory in Crisis* (Bethesda, Md.: Adler & Adler, 1985), 328-9.

26. Brand and Yancey, *Fearfully and Wonderfully Made,* 45.

27. Denton, *Evolution,* 330-1.

28. J. L. Dagg, *Manual of Theology* (1857, reprint, Harrisonburg, Va.: Gano Books, 1982), 87.

29. C. H. Spurgeon, *The Treasury of David, An Expository and Devotional Commentary on the Psalms* (Grand Rapids: Baker, 1984), 5:29.

30. Calvin, *Institutes of the Christian Religion,* 1:202.

31. Young, *The Book of Isaiah,* 3:383.

32. Dagg, *Manual of Theology,* 91.

33. Don Matzat, *Christ Esteem* (Eugene, Ore.: Harvest House, 1990), 41.

34. Matzat, *Christ Esteem,* 42.

35. Benjamin Breckinridge Warfield, *The Works of B. B. Warfield: Perfectionism, Part 1* (Grand Rapids: Baker, 1931), 7:113-4.

36. Sinclair Ferguson, *Grow in Grace* (Colorado Springs: NavPress, 1984), 36.

Scripture Index